KINFOLK

info@kinfolk.com
www.kinfolk.com

Kinfolk Magazine
5210 N Williams Avenue
Portland, Oregon 97217 USA
Telephone: 503-946-8400
Printed in Canada

Publication Design by Charlotte Heal
Cover Photograph by Neil Bedford

MADE & CRAFTED™
LEVI'S®

TOAST

TOA.ST

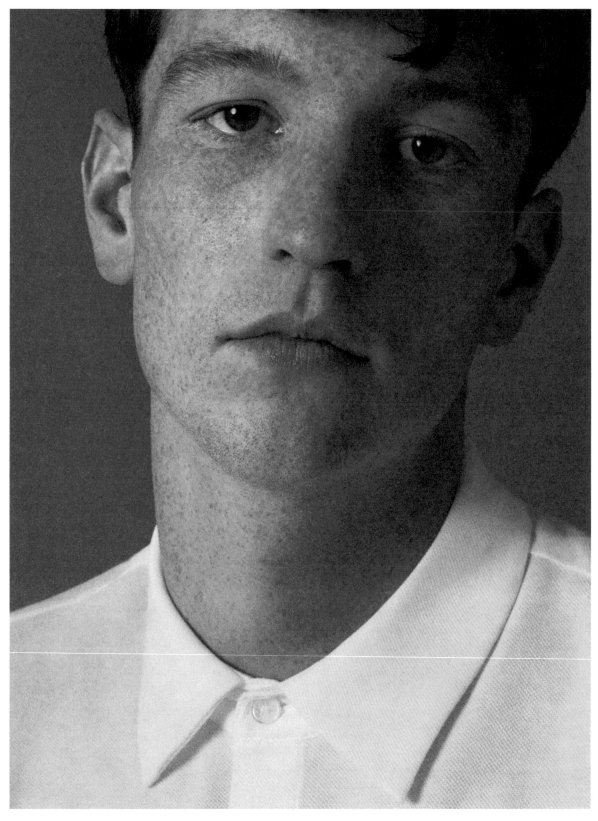

SUNSPEL

ENGLAND 1860

NATHAN WILLIAMS
Editor in Chief & Creative Director

GEORGIA FRANCES KING
Editor

ANJA VERDUGO
Art Director

GAIL O'HARA
Deputy Editor

CHARLOTTE HEAL
Design Director

DOUG BISCHOFF
Business Operations

KATIE SEARLE-WILLIAMS
Business Manager

NATHAN TICKNOR
Operations Manager

AMY WOODROFFE
Publishing Director, Ouur

JESSICA GRAY
Communications Director, Ouur

JENNIFER JAMES WRIGHT
Design Director, Ouur

PAIGE BISCHOFF
Accounts Payable & Receivable

JESSE HIESTAND
Web Administrator

AMANDA JANE JONES
Founding Designer

JOANNA HAN
Contributing Editor

ANDREA SLONECKER
Recipe Editor

KELSEY SNELL
Proofreader

RACHEL EVA LIM
Editorial Assistant

KELSEY E. THOMAS
Editorial Assistant

MEGAN HANLEY
Art Assistant

LUCIA SEKOFF
Operations Assistant

SUBSCRIBE
KINFOLK IS PUBLISHED FOUR TIMES A YEAR
TO SUBSCRIBE, VISIT WWW.KINFOLK.COM/SUBSCRIBE OR EMAIL US AT SUBSCRIBE@KINFOLK.COM

CONTACT US
IF YOU HAVE QUESTIONS OR COMMENTS, PLEASE WRITE TO US AT INFO@KINFOLK.COM
FOR ADVERTISING INQUIRIES, GET IN TOUCH AT ADVERTISING@KINFOLK.COM

www.kinfolk.com

ISSUE Nº
FOSSIL
1954

CALLING ALL CURIOUS
WWW.FOSSIL.COM

ISSUE SEVENTEEN CONTRIBUTORS

JUSTIN AARON
Photographer
Newcastle, Australia

ROSE FORDE
Stylist
London, United Kingdom

PETER MILLER
Writer
Seattle, Washington

CHANTAL ANDERSON
Photographer
Los Angeles, California

ANNE FULLERTON
Writer
Sydney, Australia

MIKKEL MORTENSEN
Photographer
Copenhagen, Denmark

NEIL BEDFORD
Photographer
London, United Kingdom

REBECCA HERNANDEZ
Prop Stylist
London, United Kingdom

BERTIL NILSSON
Photographer
London, United Kingdom

AUSTIN BRYANT
Writer
Boston, Massachusetts

DAISY HILDYARD
Writer
London, United Kingdom

SANDA VUCKOVIC PAGAIMO
Photographer
Lisbon, Portugal

RACHEL CAULFIELD
Stylist
London, United Kingdom

CARL HONORÉ
Writer
London, United Kingdom

SIDSEL RUDOLPH
Stylist
Copenhagen, Denmark

LIZ CLAYTON
Writer
Brooklyn, New York

KRISTOFER JOHNSSON
Photographer
Stockholm, Sweden

ANDERS SCHØNNEMANN
Photographer
Copenhagen, Denmark

KATRIN COETZER
Illustrator
Cape Town, South Africa

MIKKEL KARSTAD
Food Stylist
Copenhagen, Denmark

KELSEY SNELL
Writer
Brooklyn, New York

ARADIA CROCKETT
Stylist
London, United Kingdom

STEPHANIE ROSENBAUM KLASSEN
Writer
Sonoma, California

ANNU SUBRAMANIAN
Writer
New Delhi, India

MAJA DANIELS
Photographer
London, United Kingdom

CHRISTOPHE LOUIS
Illustrator
Colombes, France

DOMINIK TARABANSKI
Photographer
New York, New York

TRAVIS ELBOROUGH
Writer
London, United Kingdom

CHRIS LOW
Photographer
Portland, Oregon

ALPHA VOMERO
Stylist
New York, New York

MARGARET EVERTON
Writer
Portland, Oregon

VERONICA MARTIN
Writer
Portland, Oregon

CHIDY WAYNE
Illustrator
Barcelona, Spain

MAIA FLORE
Photographer
Paris, France

ADRIENNE MATEI
Writer
Vancouver, BC, Canada

DIANA YEN
Writer
New York, New York

extra-ordinary

ALFI by JASPER MORRISON
Made in America of 100% reclaimed industrial
waste and responsibly sourced local wood.
Read more at emeco.net

Photo: Romain Bernardie James

www.lapaz.pt

LA PAZ

WELCOME

Our concept of family is deeply personal and forever evolving. For some, it could mean mom's knowing glances, your partner's gentle chiding or grandpa's turkey gravy. For others, it could be found across the hedge you share with your neighbor, in the reciprocal banter you relish with friends or the unrequited love you have for your cat. The common thread is that the people we consider to be our family encourage us, teach us and care for us, for better or worse, in sickness and in health, till death do us part (or at least until our childhood bedrooms get turned into guest rooms).

The Family Issue of *Kinfolk* explores the relationships we have with our nearest and dearest, in all of their iterations. We ask some big questions: How is photography changing the way we construct our family narratives? Should we feel guilty about speaking to our barista more than our sister? And did our parents actually have *any idea* what they were doing? Each family has its ups and downs, but by recognizing the imperfect nature of our ties, we can work to better both our relationships and ourselves. As George Bernard Shaw said, "If you cannot get rid of the family skeleton, you may as well make it dance."

Eating together is one of the most enjoyable ways to connect with our loved ones. And it turns out there's a word for it: *commensality*. We interviewed some of the editors who quite literally wrote the book on the subject, *Commensality: From Everyday Food to Feast*, and spoke to Peter Miller, author of *Lunch at the Shop: The Art and Practice of the Midday Meal*, about the benefits of sharing a sandwich with your coworkers.

After tossing and turning about what menu to dish up (Grandma's meat loaf, three ways! Root vegetables for our roots!), we settled on the goriest of them all: the Blood Menu. But instead of it being all rare meat and bone broth, we've used red wine, pomegranate juice and oozy chocolate red velvet cakes to present an entirely vegetarian version.

In other parts of the issue, bonds are bonded, playgrounds are played in and names are named. We play I-Spy on a road trip with a band of brothers, explore the different ways to stay connected far from home and debunk the fibs and fables we were fed as kids (watermelon-seed bellies, anyone?). Friends show us different ways of weaving familial ties, such as the Taiwan-born designers of Swedish studio Afteroom and a pair of identical twin sisters in Paris who share everything from their clothes to their apartment, meals, work and friends.

This brings up an interesting thought: If two people share the same DNA as well as their upbringing, then what exactly is it that differentiates their personalities, talents and traits? In our profile series for this issue, the Creative Gene, we interviewed photographers, writers, directors, chefs, board game designers, architects and other creatives whose work deals with the concept of family. We asked them about their own childhoods and if they believe nature or nurture contributed most to their creative career paths, and we even queried a Yale researcher to see if there's any scientific evidence either way.

What we discovered is that there are as many possibilities for the way we turn out as adults as there are child-raising philosophies, educational systems and organic leather baby bootie makers (there really are *a lot* of the latter, too). No matter what kind of family we come from or the type of family we want to create ourselves, there's no longer a universal concept of "normal." There's no ubiquitous manual to consult, rules to follow or boxes to check. Well, maybe just a few: love, understanding, empathy and support. And perhaps a little patience.

NATHAN WILLIAMS AND GEORGIA FRANCES KING

Community

The folks that make up our familial communities extend beyond our traditional kin, be it our neighbors, friends, workmates, bandmates, baristas or the chap we see on the bus every day.

Home

No matter who's gathered around the dinner table—children, housemates, partners or pets—the people we share our domestic lives with greatly influence the warmth of the living situations we create.

Work

It's not uncommon to spend more time with our colleagues than with our relatives. By fostering these relationships, they can flourish into something deeper than watercooler conversations.

Play

Ball pits and board games don't have to be reserved for children: Reverting to a childlike state of mind can open our imaginations, ignite our curiosity and remind us of simpler, nostalgic times.

Food

Sharing a meal is one of the best ways to strengthen bonds. The lessons (and recipes) we learn standing alongside our elders in the kitchen are passed down through generations as an edible legacy.

NATHAN WILLIAMS
THE KINFOLK HOME
THE KINFOLK HOME
INTERIORS for SLOW LIVING
NATHAN WILLIAMS

The Kinfolk Home:
Interiors for Slow Living

———

Our second book explores 35 homes across the globe that embody the values of slow living. The families we visited share their thoughts about how to create homes built around what matters most.

Slow living means something personal to each of us, and one of the strongest ways we manifest these beliefs is by expressing ourselves through our homes. In 2013, we published *The Kinfolk Table: Recipes for Small Gatherings*, and for our second book, *The Kinfolk Home: Interiors for Slow Living*, we set out to visit 35 diverse homes across five continents that embody the slow-living principles of their inhabitants. Instead of asking these old friends, new friends and mentors to talk about the color of paint on their walls, we invited them to share their values, how those ideals have shaped their homes and how their homes have in turn shaped them.

A home isn't just a physical structure, but also a structure of our beliefs. While "living essentially" can make us think of bare bookshelves or an empty wardrobe containing only white cotton T-shirts, we're able to invite slowness and simplicity into our days without prescribing to a predetermined aesthetic; this is because slow living is less of a style and more of a deeply personal mentality.

Each space we visited speaks to its residents' innermost beliefs and reveals their character, whether it's through a collection of inherited French antiques, a table long enough for a dinner party of a dozen, a smattering of children's sketches pasted on the walls or the absence of objects in a minimal space reserved for creative thought. At the heart of each space is an aesthetic shaped by the dweller's idea of what brings joy and meaning to a home. We believe that this intention is the most important aspect of slow living.

While our homes can function as places we retreat to, we also seek to connect within them. In this way, they become active participants in our lives—living organisms that grow and shrink and change, just as we do. Perhaps this is why that feeling of "home" follows us from space to space as our street addresses change: While the outward expressions of our dwellings change form, their foundations—the people we share them with—stay the same.

In *The Kinfolk Home*, we're invited into a variety of communities: Some live with a life partner, others cohabit with a sprawling family and some prefer a humble party of one. Whatever form these communities take, home acts as a place where people can come together and become closer. Forming our spaces with this in mind strengthens the relationships that flourish under our roofs.

The ways we choose to cultivate our communities are as varied as the assortments of people they support: It could mean hosting elaborate Saturday brunches for your friends, late-summer barbecues for your neighbors or savoring an indulgent dinner cross-legged on the floor, blissfully alone. It could mean knocking out walls to open up your kitchen or adding walls for moments of private sanctuary. It could mean longer tables for even longer evenings. It could mean anything that means something to you.

Although there are many ways to create slow lifestyles, we've divided the book into three sections that these spaces epitomize: homes that cultivate community, homes that simplify our lives and homes that allow us to live slowly and with intention. Each home shares the spirit of all three, but we've allotted every one a chapter that captures the principles of each family, and we've also provided some in-depth reading material to elaborate on their messages.

We sincerely thank everyone involved for opening up their doors, their minds and often their pantries to show us how they express slow living; it has been a pleasure. The residences we visited may differ when it comes to their sizes, inhabitants, locations and aesthetics, but they all share one common denominator: Each one is a vessel not for style, but for living.

The Kinfolk Home: Interiors for Slow Living (Artisan Books) will be available for preorder in September 2015. For more details and to purchase a copy, please visit www.thekinfolkhome.com.

"*The Kinfolk Home* explores the slow living movement from a global perspective, presenting tours of creatively conceived domestic environments from Tokyo to Toronto. Featuring stunning photography and thought-provoking essays, the book is a reexamination of what it means to live small and conscientiously."

—

Julie Carlson, editor in chief of *Remodelista*

Starters

WORDS
ANNE FULLERTON

The Families
We Choose

*There's no such thing as a perfect family.
Regardless of what kind of family you were
born into, you can keep adding characters
to your clan, whether or not you're related.*

The phrase "family values" often conjures images of a cheesy half hour of prime-time television replete with big hair, wacky neighbors and lessons quickly learned. In reality, the likelihood of belonging to a family unit comprised of a goofy dad who tinkers in the garage, a mom who makes pancakes every morning and a set of slightly precocious suburban kids who never get fat (despite living on a diet of pancakes) is pretty low. In fact, in 2013 only 19 percent of U.S. households were made up of a married couple with kids. The other 81 percent of us surround ourselves with people who break the narrow mold traditionally accompanied by laugh tracks, and some of our nearest and dearest aren't related to us at all.

In reality, the friend who always answers our calls, the barista who doubles as our therapist, the hairdresser who knows our mood better than we do and the coworker who invited us out during our first crushingly lonely week in a new city can feel as much like our family as the clan we're born into. These people aren't assigned to us, but chosen by us—and isn't that as worthy of celebration as any confluence of fate and genetics? These carefully selected families continue to grow throughout our lives without a ticking sociological or biological clock to worry about.

The decline of the nuclear family is sometimes seen as a modern phenomenon, but if you dig deeply into the cultural traditions of the not-so-distant past, it's clear that family has always been an abstract concept more than a unifying description. In fact, it's the white-picket-fence model that's the anomaly.

Until the mid-1800s, a Japanese family unit was defined as a collection of people who worked together in a single village, while in Ghana, the Caribbean and Polynesia, it's not unusual for children to be fostered to other families, which means ties are often extended beyond the immediate clan. During the Middle Ages, European men were even able to join themselves to each other in a form of "sworn kinship," complete with an exchange of vows and a ceremony. King James I and his "best friend," the Duke of Buckingham, blurred familial distinctions dramatically by referring to each other as god-sibling, father, child, husband and wife.

Likewise, in other countries, terms such as *brother, sister, aunt, uncle* and *cousin* are used as expressions of endearment and respect, unrelated to genetics. Even the origin of the word *family* (Latin for *household*) seems ill-fitting at a time when more people than ever live alone or move away from the place they're born, whether it's for work, love or adventure.

Nowadays, a family is simply a network of people who care for each other. It can contain hundreds or two. You can be born into one or build your own. Membership can be gained through genetics, friendship, geographic proximity, work or a shared appreciation of *The Bachelor*. Someone who encourages your talents, cushions your heartaches, tolerates your complaints and laughs at your jokes—or even if they laugh at your complaints and tolerate your jokes—can feel as close to a brother or sister as anyone you share DNA or a dinner table with.

In our current society, real family values have nothing to do with where we live or how we know each other—they're about how we treat each other. Now *there's* a concept worthy of a cheesy half hour of television.

WORDS
AUSTIN BRYANT

From Everywhere and Nowhere

Who do you think you are? Digging up our family tree's roots can help us realize that we're all far more connected than we ever could have imagined.

Being able to recall the names and locations of the generations before us is a common desire that connects us to our personal histories. But while many of my friends could divulge details as specific as a coat of arms, I didn't know a lot of facts about my own ancestors. We knew about my mother's German heritage—we even have a map marking where our ancestors lived in Rothenburg and elsewhere across Bavaria—but my father's African-American background was murkier, as is the case with many other black Americans whose ancestry was blurred by slavery's erasing swipe. In my mind, I thought that knowing specifically where the blood in my veins came from would fill a void in my life. Not knowing the past made me feel slightly disconnected, even though I had—and deeply loved—the family right in front of me.

People had previously taken guesses at my ethnicity: Moroccan, Dominican, Egyptian, South African, Native American and other colorful hypotheticals. Years later, my family was given the chance to learn about our faceless lineage when one of my younger brothers was given an ancestry DNA test for Christmas. A cheek swab and six to eight weeks of waiting was all it took. When the results came back, it was overwhelming: Nigeria, Germany, Ivory Coast, Benin, Togo, Cameroon, Ghana, Finland, Ireland and the Iberian Peninsula. The report listed DNA percentages of heredity from each country in descending order to the point of single and seemingly inconsequential digits.

After my brother and I read through the results, there was a shared sense of "Well, I guess that's that." The information I'd wanted for so long was in front of me, but I didn't have the grand epiphany I was expecting. I'd thought that once I knew where I was from, I'd feel an instant feeling of gratification—as if a long-sought-after prize was now mine. Instead, it felt like we were from everywhere and nowhere, all at the same time.

People get so caught up in the past, expecting it to feel completely theirs. But it took this affirmation for us to realize that we're all connected in endless ways. Regardless of our nationality or proximity, this interconnectivity defines us. Whether learning about the origins of ourselves and our friends or just pondering the histories of the strangers around us, we can quietly wonder about our common bonds. It's just as possible that we share origins with any number of random tourists wandering through Times Square in New York as we do with our distant cousins.

If we occasionally reminded ourselves of this sense of connectedness, it's possible the world would seem a whole lot smaller. Many of the same struggles, passions and doubts we experience personally are repeated in the lives of others all over the world. And just because we don't share blood doesn't mean that connection is any less meaningful. Holding up a mirror to the past shows more than the reflection of our personal heritage: It also reflects our global ancestry and how we fit into the rest of the world.

WORDS
GAIL O'HARA

Ya'aburnee

Some of us would rather stop
breathing than lose the one
we love. This Arabic expression
takes that sentiment literally.

LANGUAGE: Levantine Arabic
PRONUNCIATION: "Yu'burni"
ETYMOLOGY: Arabic slang/colloquial—this phrase is used mostly in conversations in Syria, Lebanon and Palestine.
MEANING: Can you imagine loving a person so much that you'd want to die before they do because you wouldn't want to live without them? This Arabic phrase basically translates to "you bury me," meaning there's no way I'd want to go on after you're gone, darling.
USE: You would say "ya'aburnee" (also spelled "ya'arburnee") if you're declaring your feelings to a man, or you'd utter "ta'aburnee" to a woman. This would likely be spoken softly to your paramour in private rather than something you'd yell back to mom and dad casually at the airport (unless you're going away for a really, really long time).

WORDS
MARGARET EVERTON

The Art of Winging It

When we were little, our parents
often seemed like demigods, but
at some point it became clear
that they're only human.

There comes a time when most adults look back at childhood and suddenly realize that their parents had *absolutely no idea what they were doing*. Broccoli blackmail? Behavior bribes? Barricaded bedrooms? While we may have viewed our all-knowing parents as the ones with all the answers as children, our more mature selves have come to understand the fallibility of even the wisest souls. Despite how assured we think our parents might have seemed, it's now painfully apparent that they were just winging it (most of the time).

No mountain of manuals could have prepared our parents for the intricacies of dealing with actual tiny individuals. Books can suggest ways to burp a fussy baby or dislodge a pea from a toddler's nose: These are straightforward hassles, but what about when your three-year-old self innocently (and mortifyingly) pinched strangers' butts, pointed at people with eye patches or asked your aunt why she had a beard? Or how were they to know what to say when you first had your heart broken or got sat down for The Talk?

There's no protocol for such situations, but identifying and believing in an overall purpose can make uncharted territory less threatening. If asked by well-meaning relatives about their intentions, our parents probably mumbled definitive yet vague phrases such as "to create independent, loving adults" or "to raise non-psychopaths." Instead of offering the answers, they simply offered their best selves, boldly advancing step-by-step, blunder-by-blunder.

And they didn't always get it right. They grounded us for innocent curfew breaks, pushed when we *didn't want to talk about it* and snuck love notes into our lunches—in high school. We mercilessly chided them for such misnomers, and they worked to constantly refine as they went along. These missteps now glimmer with the cumulative brilliance of someone who was consistently giving their best effort.

F. Scott Fitzgerald once advised his daughter to not worry about failure, disappointments or mosquitoes. By taking cues from how our parents raised us, we can forgo the ideal and instead try for excellence. Perfection, that smug foe of any individualized endeavor, often equates flawlessness with success. But rather than becoming paralyzed by the enormity of the task before us, whether it's raising children or assembling a new tent in the dark, we can commit to doing our best while exploring the possibilities that mistakes and failures offer.

Now that we're grown-ups, we can apply this brazen, organic outlook to our lives in order to worry less about knowing exactly what we're doing before starting projects or fully living our lives. If we waited until we had all the answers, no one would ever become parents, start a business, cook a new dish or dare to ponder the intricacies of the universe. Instead, if we work to break through the restraints of the unknown, we can discover our capacity to engage life with bold creativity. Which is probably what our blundering parents were trying to teach us in the first place.

The Creative Impulse

Is creativity something everyone is born with or something we learn from our environment? We interview Yale researcher Mei Tan to find out what position science takes.

Ever wondered if your lack of artistic ability was due to your parents' mathematical-minded genetics or their refusal to sign you up for after-school art classes? Or how your friend was a piano prodigy despite her dad barely being able to play a note? Some believe that hereditary factors are responsible for one family producing generations of musical virtuosos, while others suggest that our cultural and environmental surroundings play a larger role than genetics. Mei Tan, a researcher at Yale's Child Study Center, investigates the development of cognitive skills and abilities that contribute to fostering creativity and intelligence in kids. She offers us some tips on how we can all maximize our creative capacities.

IS CREATIVITY AN INHERENT PART OF HUMAN NATURE?

Human nature is a broad term that encompasses many qualities. Creativity is less a general or amorphous quality and more a very specific capacity to exercise a specific set of skills. Is everyone born with the potential to develop these skills? I'd say yes. How these skills are called into service and developed depend on the interaction of many factors, such as personality, the family environment and often the educational environment. Creativity emerges from a complex soup of genes and situations that change as we grow and move from one stage of life to another.

HOW DO YOU SCIENTIFICALLY DEFINE CREATIVITY?

We define it as a set of skills that allow an individual to produce something that's both novel [original] and task-appropriate [useful]. It can be argued that originality and usefulness may vary depending on situations and cultures, so therefore a universal measuring stick for creativity would be impossible.

HOW DOES CULTURE IMPACT CREATIVITY'S SOCIAL VALUE?

Culture enables creativity to be recognized in society. What is recognized as creative genius is within the hands of cultural institutions, which recognize and acknowledge creativity by giving awards, calling attention to work or affixing large dollar values to various creative productions within the arts and the sciences. So culture is what ultimately defines what's valued as creative.

OGILVY & MATHER ADVERTISING EXECUTIVE THAM KHAI MENG ONCE WROTE THAT, "WE ARE ALL BORN CREATIVE. WE JUST GOT IT EDUCATED OUT OF US." DO YOU AGREE OR DISAGREE?

It's true that in some environments, the practice of creative skills isn't encouraged and may be actively discouraged. In some places, schools may present such environments. A child's immediate environment can play an important role in fostering creativity, since creativity requires opportunities to explore, experience new things and create in open-ended situations. If parents can provide more opportunities for this, that would help.

WHAT PERSONALITY TRAITS ENCOURAGE CREATIVE BEHAVIOR?

The literature on creativity suggests that there are at least a few personality traits that promote creative behavior, such as openness, a willingness to take risks and an ability to tolerate ambiguity and cope with novel situations.

HOW DID YOUR PARENTS INFLUENCE YOUR CAREER PATH?

They were both Chinese immigrants to America—my father was a mechanic and my mother took care of the family. They taught me to work hard, take opportunities, accept responsibility and eschew cowardice, less by explicit direction and more by implicit influence.

CAN WE BECOME CREATIVE BY PUTTING OUR MINDS TO IT?

People who have a difficult time differentiating one musical note from another may have a hard time singing on key. However, there are ways of overcoming or compensating for this. The plasticity of the brain is quite amazing. Necessity is indeed an effective mother of invention—motivation and exercising a clever and concentrated approach are needed to succeed at something that's difficult. It's not enough to try to draw a tree every day; figuring out what makes the tree hard to draw and tackling that persistently—perhaps by finding a new way to draw it or see it differently—is more the core of the problem. We generally develop skills as we need them. And being creative is sometimes what a person needs to be.

Read a series of interviews about creativity and family on page 128.

PHOTOGRAPH: MAIA FLORE

WORDS
CARL HONORÉ

Team Building

_Regardless of coordination, being part of
a team can teach us about compromise
and sacrifice as well as help us unwind._

Every Wednesday evening in a gym in south London, a bunch of Canadian expats gather to play ball hockey. It's a raucous return to our roots, but it's something else too: Chasing a ball around together every week has transformed a gaggle of bankers, designers, techies, lawyers, teachers and diplomats into a team. It's a regular gathering of kindred spirits that helps us face both the world and ourselves.

You might have something similar in your own life. Perhaps you play pickup kickball on weekends in a coed league, go sailing with the same crew every Saturday or take part in a pub quiz on Tuesday evenings. Whatever our chosen activity, many of us belong to a band of brothers—or sisters—united not by blood but by a shared extracurricular passion (such as channeling Michael Jordan).

Standard-issue socializing such as movie watching or bar bantering may help us bond with friends and colleagues, but playing together on a team does something more. Striving toward a shared goal (sometimes by taking on a common foe) acts as a catalyst that peels away our defenses and forges a deeper kind of trust and camaraderie. By the same token, many schools are embracing team-based learning, workplaces have started to resemble surrogate families and a whole industry now exists to foster team building and staff bonding inside companies (paintball, anyone?).

People have always created groupings beyond their clan, but now we seem to be seeking these extrafamilial relationships more than ever. Perhaps it's because the social landscape is changing: Our mobile, world-wandering lifestyles pull us away from blood relatives, creating the need for new tribes. And the trend toward having children later—or not at all—means we're spending more time in our twenties and thirties cultivating stroller-free social circles.

By serving as another family, teams can also free us from the stultifying effect of the real thing. Even healthy, happy families have a habit of stuffing their members into permanent pigeonholes. Regardless of how many years pass or how much you evolve and accomplish, when you go home for the holidays, you're often placed straight back into the same old role—you're the Joker, the Peacemaker, the Pretty One, the Slob.

Unlike these posses of preordained personas, a team is a family where no one knows what you looked like in high school or cares how many vegetables you refused to eat as a toddler. It offers a fresh start, a blank canvas, a chance to experiment with other identities and ways of being and behaving. At their best, teams do exactly what our own families are supposed to do: They make us feel rooted, safe, understood and cherished. They help us to find the best version of ourselves, and they inspire us to raise our game.

No one on my hockey team still dreams of making the big leagues, but we all turn up every Wednesday night like hungry draft prospects anyway. Why? Because we love the game, of course. But also because when we walk onto that court, with sticks in our hands, we feel like we've come home.

ILLUSTRATIONS: CHIDY WAYNE

WORDS
VERONICA MARTIN

Turning the Tables

*Tables have always played a significant role
in the way we come together to eat and create,
even if their forms and functions have changed.*

Throughout the ages, our appetites have evolved from simply needing to eat to wanting to dine. As the ways and reasons we break bread have changed, the shapes and sizes of our tables have developed to suit our tastes: Whether the surface is a round one that reminds us of our childhood kitchen, a communal one that encourages us to knock knees with strangers in restaurants or an intimate one set for two, a table's size, shape and context has everything to do with the way we interact around it.

The table and its settings have evolved over time, reflecting revolutions in manufacturing, free time, wealth, art and knowledge. In the 1300s, when early tables weren't yet permanent fixtures in the home, the phrase "to set the table" didn't refer to laying down cutlery and place mats: It meant to set a simple board on four legs. Before anything as formal as dinner tables were used, some early cultures, such as the ancient Egyptians, reportedly dined using ceramic dishware placed directly on the floor, and it's been said that the ancient Greeks often used thick, hearty bread instead of utensils or napkins. Centuries later, the ornate tables of the Baroque period mirrored the decadent spreads that were laid upon them, and the classic tables of the café society in Paris in the late 19th century—small, round and almost utilitarian—accentuated their purpose as vehicles for the creation of ideas instead of lavish meals.

In fact, before they were used for dining, tables were used as centers of creativity. The old English word *tabele* originally meant

"writing tablet," ancient Egyptians used them to elevate artifacts off the ground and the Chinese were the first to use them as surfaces for drawing and painting. And this trend has continued through modern times: In the 1920s, a circle of literary luminaries such as Dorothy Parker and Robert Benchley frequently met for lunch at Manhattan's Algonquin Hotel, forming a band of writers known as the Round Table. Guests at their gatherings included stars such as Harpo Marx and Ernest Hemingway—the latter reportedly wrote one of the most famous micro-stories in history after someone at the table bet him that he couldn't write a story in six words or less: "For Sale, Baby Shoes, Never Worn." Nicknaming themselves the "Vicious Circle," the writers created a community around this table—one with its own language and wit, where individuals came together to challenge each other's creative output.

These days, tables have come to represent a surface where sustenance and creation come together—a place to wonder and to solve problems, to probe and to redefine our roles. It stands as a symbol of our connectedness with each other and with ourselves: We come to eat, we stay to dine. In this way, the table has become a site where our lives play out and where we draw ideas and narratives into existence. How we set the table, how we spend time at the table and who we choose to share the table with directly reflects the way we live away from the table—change one, and you'll inevitably change the other.

WORDS
MARGARET EVERTON

A State of Solitude

Just because you shared personal space as a kid doesn't mean you need to give up your individuality as an adult: Carving time out for yourself can strengthen your family ties.

Whether our family life is gloriously ideal or quietly chaotic, we all need to carve out a space of our own. Family gatherings—not to mention families in general—can be energetic and emotional, often prompting us to sacrifice the sense of self we usually fiercely protect for the greater good. While enthusiastic participation and personal downtime might seem at odds, interweaving the two can create a much more effective way of engaging with our loved ones.

Even the most altruistic of humans can become flat-out exhausted by the social nature of family life. During childhood we're taught to be independent individuals, yet adult family time often stirs an oddly paradoxical expectation to share everything. "Even prison gives you some personal space, so why not family?" a friend once quipped. We probably never spent this much time together when we lived under the same roof—and loyalty should not require us to quell our independence and spend every minute with each other now.

One of the best ways to preserve personal space can be to simply slip away from the crowd. If we get an urge to snap at our dads or pinch our sisters, the best course is often to remove yourself from the situation at hand to retreat and regroup. Simple solitary activities such as taking a walk after breakfast—or skipping it altogether to read in bed—can help restore our calm composure. Other solutions for alone time include using an evening to disappear in the garden, slipping away for an afternoon nap or opting to stay in a nearby hotel rather than our old bedroom. While some may protest our absences, these acts of self-preservation can prolong and strengthen family life itself over time.

Tension can run high even at the happiest of rendezvous, and calmly observing group edginess is often the most positive way to stay involved. We don't need to act as peacekeeper for the Corporation of Family Conviviality to encourage esprit de corps over melodrama. Instead of adding another voice to the chorus, we can offer tranquility and wisdom through silence. You can passively disregard when your big brother goads you with that idiotic nickname or your mother tries to "arrange" your hair. You can be blasé in the midst of an impromptu, unimportant feud and shrug and sip coffee when asked to take sides.

But sometimes preservation calls for a stronger assertion of self. Boldness might be less comfortable than conformity, but it gives a family the chance to know and love us accurately. As writer Henry Miller suggested, "Clarify your position!" That yes, you adopted *another* dog! That you're now vegetarian, homemade meat loaf or no homemade meat loaf! That you're not getting married, ever! And if your disclosures don't exactly go over smoothly, at least you'll leave the gathering with a firm sense of satisfaction knowing you were wholly yourself.

Being part of a group while giving ourselves personal space is one of life's biggest challenges. Our families have always known us and, while they might be our greatest supporters, they often forget that we need room to expand in the same way we once outgrew our training wheels. We might opt out of meals, disappear during the annual family movie or decline another round of poker, but when we reengage, it's with zeal. Caring passionately about our families is essential, but we must first care for ourselves.

COMPILED BY
THE KINFOLK TEAM

Our Given Names

The monikers our parents gave us can have an interesting impact on our childhoods. We ask some friends about the meanings of their names and how they've influenced their identities.

LISLE WINSTON

I used to hate my weird name: All I wanted was a normal one so that I could go into a rest stop in New Jersey and buy a seashell key chain with my name on it. When I was 16, I found out about a town called Lisle in Illinois. I ended up writing a very long letter addressed to Lisle High School about how cool it was to have the same name as a town with a pretty good football team, and I included a check to the Lisle Parent Teacher Association for $20 and a request for any Lisle merch. A very nice lady sent me back a handwritten letter and a "Lisle Lions" T-shirt, which I still wear proudly. Now I like that instead of sharing my name with people, I share it with a small town. I still say my name is Lila when ordering coffee though, because it's just easier that way.

CHLOE STONE RINEHART

When I was 12, I legally changed my name to Chloe Stone Rinehart. Before, it was Chloe Michael McGough: McGough was my dad's last name, and Michael was my mom's father's first name. Neither my mom nor I had particularly good relationships with our dads, so my brother and I wanted to change our last names to Rinehart, my mom's maiden name, and I also decided to change my middle name to Stone, my mom's partner's last name. (They've been together since I was seven, and she's more my other parent than my dad is.) We initially wanted to keep it a secret from mom's partner, but when the social security cards came in the mail, we showed them to her and I still remember us all crying. It was a really powerful moment. I have a lot of ownership over and pride about my name as a result, which I know can be really rare.

TOMMY EDWARD THOMAS

Before my father was born, my grandmother's brother Tommy passed away. My grandmother decided she would name her next son Tommy in his memory, despite the fact that she married a man whose last name was Thomas. Since I was my father's only son, he decided I should carry the name on for another generation. Growing up, people found the name strange and made that very clear to me. It wasn't until my freshman year of college that I began to realize how beneficial having such a unique name could be. People I met were suddenly intrigued by my name rather than confused. I was always introduced as Tommy Thomas instead of simply Tommy—it became odd to have someone refer to me as just Tommy. I've grown to appreciate being born with a conversation starter and a way into people's memory through my name alone. However, it's never easy speaking with customer service reps: *"Last name?"* "Thomas." *"First name?"* "Tommy." *"OK, and what's your last name?"* "Thomas." *"I have that, but I need your last name."* "My name is Tommy Thomas." *"Your name is Tommy Thomas?"* Every. Time.

MADELEINE GASPARINATOS

That's right, 21 juicy letters. No middle name, as I don't need more letters than that. My surname is phonetic, but people freak out about it. For a while, I thought my surname was detrimental when applying for jobs, so I've used a shortened version before: Gaspar. I don't know whether it made a difference. Now I like the multiculturalism of it and the connection to my dad's family and my Greek heritage, as my dad and grandparents have passed away. I feel really lucky to have that ethnic side so immediately obvious through my name.

PHOEBE BLUESKY SUMMERSQUASH

It was 1969 (need I say more?). My mom and her husband at the time were running a health food store and mail-order lending library in Vermont. They received a book request from Pauline Pigeon, a moniker that inspired them to dream up their own wacky new names. They agreed that Summersquash had a good-natured ring to it and went to the town clerk's office to make their new surname official. Within a year they were separated, and my mom was back in Rhode Island foraging for herbs in Swan Point cemetery. While there, she had a vision of what her not-yet-conceived daughter might look like as an adolescent and decided then and there that her name would be Phoebe Bluesky. Soon after, she met my dad and they had me. And that's the name I got. The ups of having a crazy name have definitely outweighed the downs. As a kid, it was challenging but relatively nontraumatic. I'm happy to carry on my mother's eccentric legacy. It's a name to live up to.

ROBERT "BOB" HOWARD SMITH

That's right: Bob Smith. There's actually a documentary, *Bob Smith USA*, that claims there are 82,000 of us running around America. My hunch is that number is low. As a freelance design director, I have what's most likely an unhealthy fondness for stirring the pot: I paint my nails, I let my hair go crazy, etc. The irony of being such an incorrigible troublemaker with such a generic name is kind of the perfect subterfuge—it throws people off, which of course I love.

MANON LEFÈVRE

My name is only unusual because I live in the United States. In France, Manon is one of the most common names for girls. I really appreciate it when people try to pronounce it, and I get annoyed at those who purposefully never say my name out loud in an obvious way. I've had a million terrible mispronunciations over the years, but the most memorable is still from my first-ever gym teacher in the U.S., who called me Monet, like the painter. I guess that's the only French name she'd ever heard, so she just went with that.

ZOE MARQUEDANT

I was once in a small Virginia college town having Greek food for lunch when the proprietor asked my name for my order, and I said Zoe. The guy nodded slowly and handed me a giant slice of baklava, free of charge. So the Greek thing is usually a perk. But I got real tired of people asking me what Zoe was short for in high school. I mean, what could it possibly be? Zosephine? I don't like it when people add extra vowels and/or punctuation to my name. It's not Zooey, Zoey or Zoë. Similarly when people write Zo—would you like to buy a vowel? I mean, it's three letters long—I'm not asking for much. There's definitely a big gaping hole in my heart where a nickname should've been. I never had one, and all my friends who were Elizabeths and Katherines could be called a million things. That's why I automatically nickname people nowadays—in case they've been waiting for a nickname for all these years just as I have.

CAITLIN SIMONE TANUMYROSHGI

My family name is Tanumyroshgi, which is an anagram of my parents' names. Every time I have to pick up something new, I'm grilled about it. Most people think I'm Polish, Russian or Japanese: I've found that when you have a striking name, people want to know more about it to "place you," as if understanding where someone's ancestors are from will give them an idea of who they are as a person.

MA. ELENA CECILIA "EILEEN" MONTILLA FRANCISCO

Ma. is the abbreviation for Maria—it's an old Spanish Catholic tradition used in the Philippines to name your daughter after the Virgin Mary. And yes, it's spelled with a period. When I was in South America, Latinos pronounced it correctly, referring to me as "Maria Elena" instead of just "Mah."

AARON LI-HILL

I really like my name. It's a signifier about my mixed Chinese and Austrian background, so it's made me feel like a special breed of East meets West. To further this feeling of hybridity, I was born in Canada and raised a reconstructionist Jew. My grandmother was visiting America from China right when the cultural revolution happened and tensions between the U.S. and China escalated. Her parents forced her to stay in the America, and she didn't see them for many, many years. My mother was born here, and that's where Li comes from. Originally, my father's family name was Berger, but when my Austrian grandfather enlisted in the British military, they made him change his name to Hill for fear of being tortured if he was captured by the Germans—they considered all Austrians that fought against them traitors. So that's the Hill. Having a mix of both my parents' names makes me feel proud that there's an equal representation in me instead of the normal patriarchal system that eliminates women's histories. I want to name my future child this way, but I guess down the road the names could just get really, really long.

LORELEI VASHTI WAITE

My daughter's last name is half my surname and half my partner's: Waite + Wortsman = Waitsman. It didn't feel right to either of us that kids should automatically have their dad's surnames, so we talked until we found a solution. Luckily my partner is a rad feminist who never felt attached to his surname—he's always done things his own way.

CHIARA SCAFIDI

Chiara is an Italian name that means light, clear or bright. People often say they like my name, but I seem to come up against those who refuse to understand how to say it back to me. "I'm Chiara." "*Chair?*" "Chiara." "*Tiara?*" "No, Chiara." "*Chee-ara?*" "Chiara." "*Kyara?*" One day, when ordering coffee, I had the enlightened idea of saying my name was Claire. I thought it was foolproof. When I got my to-go cup, I looked at the scrawled felt-tip name on the side. It said "Clay."

PHOTOGRAPH: MIKKEL MORTENSEN

Kinfolk's take on Øyvind's bedside table: Yeh Wall Table by Menu. Model 10 Clock Radio by Tivoli Audio. Miltzen eyeglasses by Moscot. Minima Water Glass by Cecilie Manz for Rosendahl. Mega Dot Quilt bedspread by HAY. Elephant by Kay Bojesen. Pillows by Louise Smærup (front) and Aiayu (back).

My Bedside Table:
The Illustrator

———

*As an award-winning children's book illustrator
and comic-book artist living in Oslo, Norway,
Øyvind Torseter often finds inspiration in the
moments before sleep.*

"In the morning, I make breakfast while my wife and daughters get up. We drink juice and eat bread with cheese or jam, or sometimes we'll have oat porridge with fruit and nuts. Then we follow the girls to school and I walk to my studio afterward, looking forward to getting a cup of coffee and drawing. The first two to three hours at work are sacred. I try to avoid being distracted during this time—I don't look at emails or plan any meetings before lunch. I just draw. This has been my routine for years now, and I love it.

I'm a freelancer, so in theory I could choose my own schedule, working late in the evening and getting up late, but I never do that anymore. I like my days to be ordinary, and if I work long days and sleep less, I'm not as focused. After having children, my days and evenings have become more structured, and I really like that. I now work 9 to 4, get to bed around 11 p.m. and wake up around 6 a.m. to either my radio or the kids, whichever comes first. I like the sound of the radio slowly creeping into my dreams and connecting with them.

My bedroom has a window with a view of some big trees. There are a couple of abstract, nature-form etchings on the walls, a painting of a wooden toy dog over the bed, as well as several drawings by our three daughters. One of my favorites is a picture of all of us sleeping that was drawn by my eldest daughter. I keep a lot of books and magazines near my bedside table, as well as a glass of water, a radio and my glasses.

Before bed, my wife and I have supper and maybe watch a series on TV before checking to see if the kids are fast asleep. After the house is quiet, I try to read a little before bed, but usually I'm so tired that I only read a few pages. At the moment I'm reading Lynda Barry's *What It Is* and *Picture This*, which are great books about the creative process of drawing and writing. I'm also reading some manuscripts for books that I'm illustrating. A few of my favorite illustrated works that inspire me are Tove Jansson's Moomins cartoons, *Sailor Och Pekka* by the brilliant Swedish artist Jockum Nordström and works by Swedish illustrator Jan Lööf, Wolf Erlbruch and, of course, Maurice Sendak.

Before sleeping, I try to avoid opening emails in the bedroom and I don't use my iPad as it just lights up my head. But I do have my sketchbook with me everywhere, including next to my bed. It's nice to get ideas down on paper—it's like cleaning my head before sleep. When my ideas are put to paper, I don't have to think about them so much. I make notes on all kinds of ideas, both good and bad. Sometimes ideas that are no good in your head are good when they touch the paper, and often a problem that's impossible to solve by just thinking can be solved while we're sleeping."

A Treasure Trove of Heirlooms

Every generation leaves something behind for the next to inherit. It could be precious gems, useless junk or familiar characteristics, all of which help us understand where we came from.

My grandparents once ran a pirate-themed fish restaurant in a seaside resort town in the south west of England. It was called the Jolly Roger, and it had swords on its walls and menus in heavy faux-leather binders embossed with images of sextants and compasses. Written out in an elaborate copperplate that was hard to decipher, the menus made ordering haddock feel as if you were hunting for buried treasure. And since it aspired to be a classy joint, despite the goofy decor, the restaurant provided proper fish knives.

When my grandmother died, I inherited a bunch of these fish knives and a set of accompanying forks, some of which were inscribed with Hebrew characters. They didn't look like anything you'd really want to put near your food—or in your mouth. Tarnished with the wear and tear of thousands of strangers' meals, they were made of a metal that didn't seem to be silver. I guess if I'd had first pick of the family loot (the ancestral booty, as it were), I would have preferred the swords or menus. But those were long gone, lost in a lifetime my grandparents spent doing other things. But for some reason, they curiously clung to those fish knives. I cling to them now too; a meager inheritance perhaps, but one I cherish nevertheless.

That's one of the funny things about inheritance: We rarely get to choose what we get—instead, we get what we're given. In fact, many family hand-me-downs are genetic or biological, doted upon us with no choice at all. They take the form of physical features or even character traits: Some might receive brown eyes and nearsightedness or a wheat allergy and perfect pitch. Others might end up with a remarkable ability to add up figures in their heads and an inability to get to meetings on time, or you might get a sweet tooth, a short temper and stinginess—it's a crapshoot really.

Then through an element of nurture, some parental behaviors manifest in us too. Over time, their idiosyncrasies become our idiosyncrasies, whether that means a passion for cooking, stamp collecting, Bichon Frisé dogs or an irrational hatred of green beans and burlap fabrics. And how many times have you uttered words or phrases and thought with a shudder, *Oh god, I sound just like my mother*.

The German poet Goethe once wrote that there were only two lasting bequests that parents could hope to leave to their children: One was roots, the other, wings. These passed-down features not only help make us who we are and shape the way we'll be living in the future, but they also connect us to a past whose antecedents might stretch right back to our earliest ancestors. Whatever we receive from our forbearers places us in a continuum, reminding us that someday we'll be passing our odd items and eccentric characteristics on as well. At which time, of course, someone else will still be stuck with the fish knives.

Lunch at the Shop

———

*Seattle bookshop owner
Peter Miller discusses the
meaning of sitting down for
lunch with your coworkers.*

Each afternoon, the staff at Peter Miller Architecture and Design Books in Seattle gathers to enjoy a simple lunch. In much the same way that families tend to sit together discussing their days over dinner, sharing a work-free break to munch on a meal with your coworkers can make the whole office feel more connected. Peter has compiled his communal recipes into a cookbook called *Lunch at the Shop: The Art and Practice of the Midday Meal* (Harry N. Abrams, 2014), which features dozens of recipe ideas for creating fresh meals to savor with your workmates, even on the busiest of days. He explains why sharing a meal with the folks you work with can benefit more than just your bellies:

"I started making communal lunches for my workmates nearly a decade ago. At the time the shop was near the Public Market in Seattle, which looked like a theme park of places to have lunch, but many of them were more boast than truth, and some of the better places were simply too expensive or involved more time than we had. It seemed absurd to watch each person return from a lunch foray with something different, often in a clear plastic snap-down box. In my view, the sad lunch is the lunch hunched over, not shared, taken to a corner. It's not easy to know what you have in common with other people nowadays, so lunch is an occasion to try to bridge that divide with your colleagues. We decided to make a very straightforward lunch for four people and see where that might lead.

Over time, sharing meals has brought our office together in small but significant ways. Everyone can relax for a moment and tell stories that don't get told during the rest of the workday. Food seems to break down hierarchies in the best way. It's hard to decide to make yourself a good lunch, as it can feel like a vanity. But when it involves even just one or two other people, and you put the phones away and sit for a second, then it makes some sense. I can also make a much better salad for four than for myself, and a much better soup. By sitting for a moment, you are for that time a family.

Using just a few ingredients, you can make up a lunch that will blithely waltz past the best clear-plastic-container alternative. We try to always have cooked beans, rice and pasta in the fridge—with those items, it's always possible to spruce up a soup or make the base for a salad. Depending on the season, we might leave the specifics of any meal to the last minute, especially in the summer when so much produce seems available. In the colder months, a stew, hearty soup or pasta with meatballs may be just the thing and only needs to be reheated at work. Sandwiches are fine—we make them often—but we also fool around with them a little. Soups are the easiest to share of course, and lentil soup is the best gatherer of them all.

Your greatest allies are the seasons, the weather and the details. Spring and summer are the easiest as you can simply let the fresh produce be the inspiration. Once the asparagus and peas come up, we put them on and in everything for a while. But other times you'll need to keep yourself propped up, and several things can help keep it fresh: a lovely lemon, a lime, parsley, cilantro, an orange, chutney, green sauce, and even a few frozen peas will add interest to a hot soup. The zest of a lemon can lift the weight off the heartiest, dullest stew, and lemon juice can make even the most sullen slice of fish seem fresh. A good, freshly cracked Tellicherry peppercorn will make the whole room smell of fresh pepper—good cracked pepper can save you! And fresh chives are perfect on top of every soup and salad. For some reason, a simple place mat seems to make a difference and bring a kind of order, as does a water glass, knife and fork, even if they're mismatched.

Lunch has been abused for so long—overlooked, abandoned, even resented for its interruption. No one has time. But it's a place between the front and back end of a day, and it's yours for the taking. It's important to take a break from being on alert. Stop, have a bite, look up. It's a moment of intimacy: Perhaps it's not a great, broad coming together, but a shared smile or a shared apple at least."

The Lunch Box:
White Bean Soup
with Garlic and Sausage

This recipe is adapted from Peter Miller's Lunch at the Shop, a book that encourages you to share lunch with your coworkers. It can easily be doubled for larger groups: The leftovers, if there are any, are probably the best part.

SERVES 4

AT HOME

¼ cup (60 milliliters) plus 1 tablespoon extra-virgin olive oil

2 mild Italian sausages, cut into bite-size pieces

2 cloves garlic, minced

2 cups (390 grams) dried cannellini beans, cooked and drained (see below)

Salt and freshly ground pepper

1 cup (240 milliliters) chicken stock

½ cup (10 grams) fresh flat-leaf parsley leaves, chopped

AT THE SHOP

2 tablespoons extra-virgin olive oil

COOKED BEANS

2 cups (390 grams) dried beans, soaked overnight

1 bay leaf

1 clove garlic

1 sprig thyme

1 celery stalk

½ onion

Salt

AT HOME

Heat a sauté pan over medium heat, then add 1 tablespoon of oil and heat for 1 minute. Add the sausages and cook for 6 to 8 minutes, turning them while they brown, adjusting the heat as needed. Remove them from the pan and set aside on paper towels to drain.

In a soup pot, heat the remaining ¼ cup (60 milliliters) of the oil. Add the garlic over medium heat. The temperature must be high enough to lightly cook the garlic but not so high that the garlic browns. Cook until aromatic, stirring occasionally, 2 to 3 minutes.

Add the beans, stirring them into the oil and garlic. Season with salt and pepper, and cover the pan. Cook the beans, covered, for 3 minutes to infuse the flavors, and then stir in ½ cup (120 milliliters) of the stock.

Using a slotted spoon, remove about one-third of the beans and process them through a ricer or food mill back into the pan. (You can alternatively squish the beans through a slotted spoon or mash them in a bowl.) This will thicken the soup. Stir in the remaining ½ cup (120 milliliters) stock, keeping the mixture simmering. (You might need to add a little warm water if the soup's too thick). Add the sausage and parsley, and stir to combine. Taste and adjust the seasoning.

AT THE SHOP

Before reheating, add 2 tablespoons of warm water, then stir the soup to combine everything evenly. Drizzle the top with a thin line of the oil just before serving.

COOKED BEANS

Rinse the beans, picking through and tossing any broken pieces away. Put them in a saucepan with 6 cups (1 ½ liters) of cold water, and add more if needed to cover the beans. Add the bay leaf, garlic, thyme, celery and onion: There's no need to chop them, so toss them in whole. (Don't add the salt until after they're cooked.)

Bring the water to a slow boil over medium-high heat, stirring occasionally, and then adjust the heat to maintain a low simmer. Leave the pot uncovered, and skim away the foam that collects on the surface. Add more water as needed to keep the beans covered as they cook.

The beans should be done in 45 to 60 minutes, but the many variations in bean size and age will affect cooking time, and some can take up to 2 hours to cook. Taste them every 10 minutes or so after 45 minutes. The beans should be tender but not mushy. Add salt once the beans are tender, and discard the herbs, garlic, celery and onion.

Refrigerate the beans in their cooking liquid in an airtight container if they're not being used right away. They'll keep for up to a week. Drain before using.

PHOTOGRAPH: ANDERS SCHØNNEMANN; FOOD STYLING: MIKKEL KARSTAD; PROP STYLING: SIDSEL RUDOLPH

Family

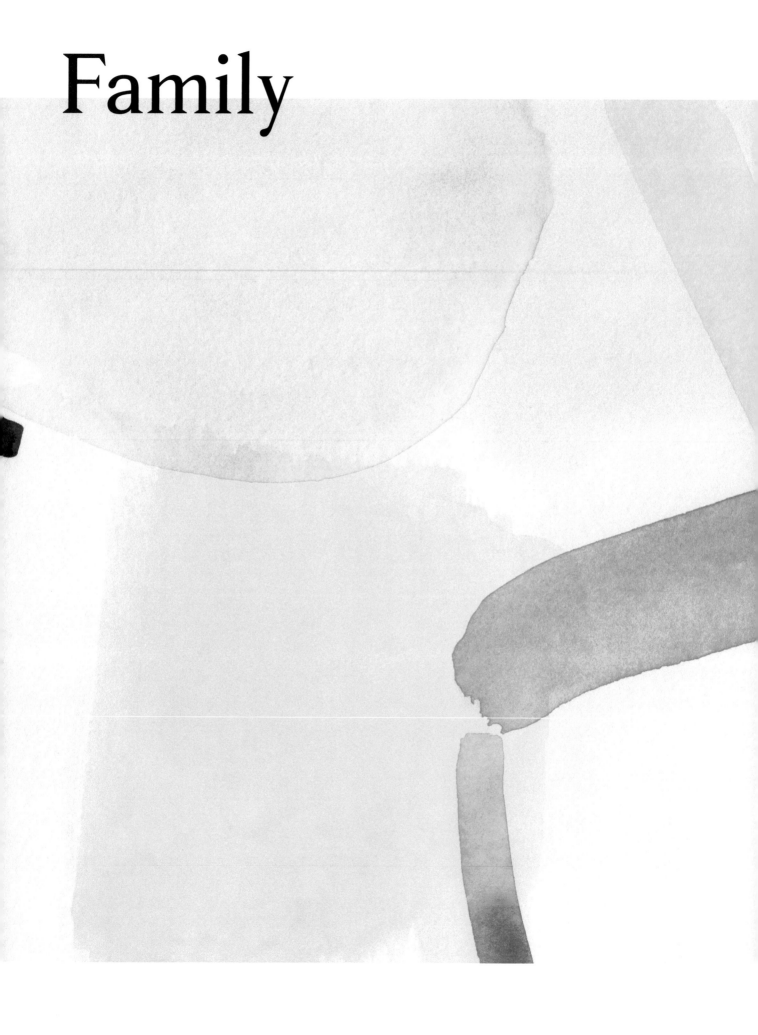

PHOTOGRAPHS
NEIL BEDFORD

STYLING
ARADIA CROCKETT

The Social Network

Mail carriers, baristas, even the girl you see regularly at your local café: These folks can go from strangers to friends in an afternoon and give you the support system you need when you're far away from family.

THE BEST FRIEND

There should be at least one person in your life who intuitively knows when
you need a giant plate of nachos, a reassuring shoulder squeeze or
a kind-but-firm reality check.

THE TEAMMATE

Whether you're shooting hoops or practicing for a pub quiz, bonding
over a common foe can fortify friendships (and sometimes win
you drink vouchers).

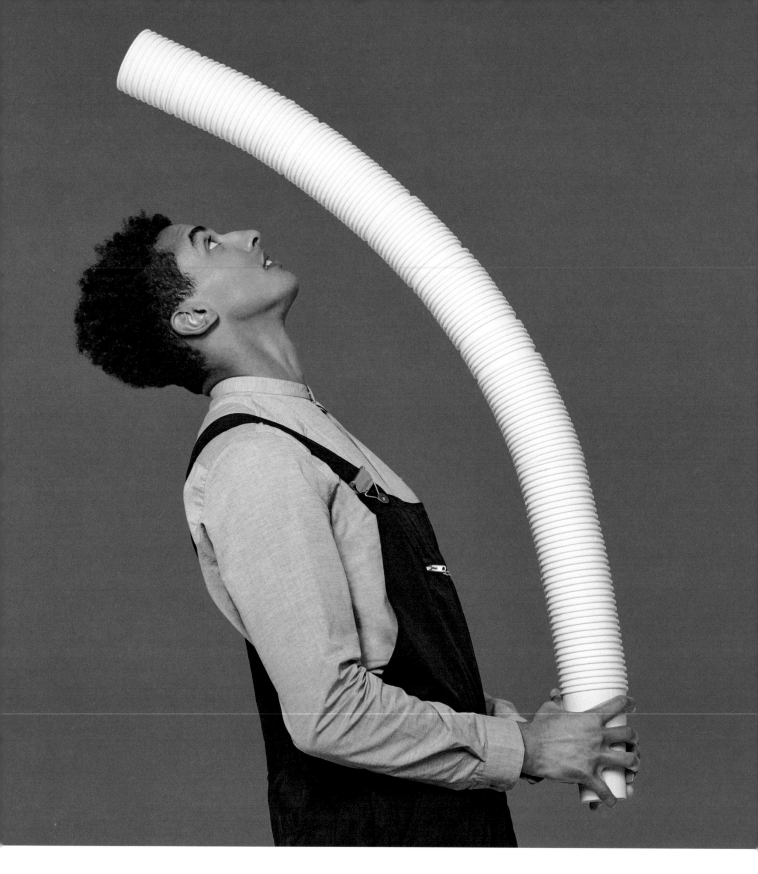

THE BARISTA

The peppy soul behind the counter is one of the few that puts up with Morning You,
knows your order by heart, understands your foggy brain and might even slip you the
occasional misshapen muffin for free.

THE HAIRDRESSER

Who needs a therapist? You're never more vulnerable than when sitting
in the hair chair, which may explain why your regular snipper always
seems to know exactly what to say.

THE BANDMATE

It doesn't matter if it's free jazz or polka you love: The person you
share a stage—or your parents' garage—with is a part of your
highest guitar-solo highs and your lowest bum-note lows.

THE MENTOR

Not only will they gladly tolerate your off-tune "Greensleeves" rendition, but having someone to teach you how to dominate a chess board, properly baste a turkey or be a better person also reminds you that there's always room to learn and grow.

THE CAT SITTER

If you deem someone trustworthy enough to watch over your real-life feline,
chances are that you'll have more in common than an affinity for watching
virtual ones on YouTube.

THE NEIGHBOR

From your serious online shopping issues to late-night Thai deliveries, the chap across the fence already knows your secrets: Fostering this connection can have benefits beyond flour-borrowing privileges and collecting each other's mail.

INTERVIEW
KELSEY E. THOMAS

PHOTOGRAPHS
KRISTOFER JOHNSSON

A Day in the Life:
Hung-Ming Chen & Chen-Yen Wei

Originally from Taiwan, Hung-Ming Chen and Chen-Yen Wei launched the Stockholm-based studio Afteroom in 2011. We spent a day with them in Sweden learning about their working process, their home life and how their folks influenced their careers.

Hung-Ming and Chen-Yen's design studio Afteroom has a philosophy based on simplicity and honesty—and it shows in both their furniture design and the way they spend their time. When the designers aren't creating items that withstand passing fads or sourcing inspiration from their local library, they prioritize playing with their seven-year-old daughter, visiting parks as a family or having a quick date in the city. They explain how they've created a home and fostered a sense of family in a Stockholm suburb far away from where they grew up.

You live in Sweden but are originally from Taiwan. When did you move away from home?
— *Chen-Yen*: We moved to Sweden in 2006 when we were in our mid-twenties. We had just gotten married when Hung-Ming decided to quit her job to further her education abroad. The main reason we came here was so she could get a master's degree in design at Konstfack [a university college for art, crafts and design]. It was a new adventure. Adapting to a different culture and lifestyle was exciting, but it also felt uneasy. Things went further than we planned: We didn't know we would stay here for as long as we have.

Have you created your own traditions away from your families? — *Chen-Yen*: I inherited many of my living habits from my family. I had a very happy childhood and the positive memories from that deeply influenced me when I had my own family. I like sharing my stories from my childhood with my daughter at bedtime, and she shares her daily story with me in return.

What has it been like visiting Taiwan after moving away? How has your relationship with your home country changed? — *Chen-Yen*: We visit Taiwan about once every two years. Since we've moved away from our hometown, every time we go back to Taiwan, we start to appreciate something we used to ignore or take for granted, such as the beautiful landscape of the mountainside or the super-convenient local breakfast bars and night markets. Bit by bit, we see it differently than we used to and we understand more about what's been deeply rooted in our subconscious, both the good and bad.

What do you miss the most about Taiwan? — *Hung-Ming*: I miss the hot springs a lot. Taiwan has dead volcanoes, so there are many places with hot springs. It only takes about a 30-minute drive from central Taipei or a train ride to the mountainside to find them. When I was working as a designer in Taiwan before moving to Sweden, we sometimes went to the mountainside right after work to enjoy the springs and eat great food.

What's your relationship with your siblings like? — *Chen-Yen*: I have one sister who's two years older than me. We have a very close relationship. I remember enjoying chatting and doing silly things together when we were little. In many ways, she was like a mentor during our childhood. Sometimes she helped me when I was having trouble with my art homework at home, since she has innate artistic talent. She also acted as a love expert and gave me advice to deal with tough situations. I'm so grateful to have had her as my spiritual backing since I was little.

Were you particularly close to anyone else in your family? — *Hung-Ming*: I was close to my grandma. She grew up during the period of time when Taiwan was managed by Japan, so she can speak good Japanese. When I was little, my parents needed to work constantly, so I was around her quite often. She used to take me to the parks and would sing Japanese songs to me. I can still vaguely remember the melodies.

How do you stay connected to your families while living far away from home? — *Hung-Ming*: We use the internet. I used to call my parents just to say hello to them via FaceTime almost every day, but somehow my mother found that quite annoying, so she told me to stop calling so frequently! However, I still send them messages often or share funny videos with them.

How has living in two different cultures shaped your idea of family? — *Hung-Ming*: The most significant difference between Taiwanese and Swedish family culture is the hierarchy. In traditional Asian culture, we obey our parents' authority. There's a clear line you should never cross and certain behavior you should follow as a child. In Sweden, on the other hand, people treat children more like friends. We like the mentality of equality here, so we hope our daughter also sees us as friends. We give her sufficient space to let her just be herself and are super-patient with her when she's out of control. But sometimes my traditional Taiwanese parent side pops out, loudly making demands and setting rules when I just want to get things done. At that point, I realize that I'm still subconsciously like a traditional Asian father, thinking I know what's best and that she should listen to me. Perhaps there's no contradiction between the two different cultures, and instead I need to find the balance between freedom and discipline. I'll probably never achieve that balance, but I'll keep trying.

How has growing up in Taiwan and now living in Sweden shaped your philosophy about home its purpose? — *Hung-Ming*: In a way, home is a kind of school without a teacher where we can continually learn about ourselves. At the same time, as designers, home is a place where we like to practice our vision and to create our own wonderland.

Left: The chairs in Chen-Yen and Hung-Ming's studio were one of their first designs and were also part of Menu's SS13 collection. They remain one of Afteroom's most popular items.

Above: Chen-Yen and Hung-Ming's love of tea inspired them to add tea-related items to their first collection. Afteroom included two traditional Taiwanese teas—Dong Ding Oolong Tea and Gui Fei Oolong Tea—in its Autumn/Winter 2012 collection.

Please describe your neighborhood and tell us what drew you there. — *Hung-Ming*: We live in Telefonplan in southwest Stockholm, about 15 minutes on the subway from the city center. Since Konstfack moved to the area in 2004, it has gradually transformed into a creative area that attracts art and design exhibitions, new start-up companies and design studios. A few years ago I was a student at Konstfack, so it was obvious for us to find a place nearby to settle down. Most of our friends in Sweden have some sort of link to Konstfack—it's like a hub for designers to connect with each other.

Please tell us a bit about your home. — *Chen-Yen*: It's a small, two-room apartment three minutes away from Konstfack. The interior is white-based, and keeping it simple makes it look bigger. I usually make an effort trying to make our living environment ideal. Even though we don't have our dream living space, I still like to make things as nice and tidy as possible. This comes from my perfectionist character, which has been shaped since I was little. Now we're gradually retiring our old IKEA furniture and replacing it with our own designs.

What do you usually cook at home? — *Chen-Yen*: I'm the chef of the house. I started to spend time in the kitchen and learned how to cook right after moving to Sweden. I usually mix Taiwanese and Swedish styles of cuisine because our daughter prefers Swedish

food while Hung-Ming and I prefer Taiwanese. However, sometimes I just create my own creative recipes that aren't like either country's style: We call it "the flavor of mama." I like to keep the kitchen clean and tidy—it's never a mess when I finish cooking. On the other hand, I always call Hung-Ming "blasting artist" if he gets the chance to use the kitchen.

Do you continue to honor any Taiwanese traditions? Have you adopted any Swedish ones? — *Hung-Ming*: In Taiwan, people bow to show respect, and I've continued to do this in Sweden, because I can't help myself! I've been taught to bow since I was little. I also exchange business cards with others in the Taiwanese way, which is a bit like the Japanese style: We bow deeply and use both hands to give away the business card. It's fun, so I keep doing it the way I always have. We like Swedish *fika*, which is a break to get coffee with cinnamon rolls or other sweet pastries at around 10:30 a.m. and 3 p.m. It boosts your energy and helps keep you in a good mood, especially during the endless freezing dark of winter.

How do you spend your weekends? — *Chen-Yen:* We choose a place where the three of us feel happy to spend time, usually around nature. Our favorite spot is Aspuddsparken, which is a lovely park with a small zoo. Every time we visit the farm animals, we feel some sort of spiritual healing effect that makes us peaceful and calm.

Above: The living room cabinet, designed by Ehlén Johansson for IKEA PS Collection in 2009, houses miscellaneous gadgets ranging from sewing tools to a first aid kit.

What do you like to do in your spare time? — *Hung-Ming:* In addition to watching movies, our daily entertainment is playing and talking with our daughter. She's now seven years old, which is a fun age. We usually make nonsense games and dance with her at home. She's an only child, so we think we should be more like her friends when playing with her, though sometimes I feel she sees me more as a toy or a form of transportation!

Since you both live and work together, how do you balance your personal and professional lives? — *Chen-Yen:* Sometimes we work separately: Hung-Ming stays in the studio close to our home, which is in the same building at Konstfack, and I work at home. It's an easy way to give each other some space. We often take a half day off during the week to take a walk in the park or go to the city for a short date to relax ourselves and get some inspiration on the street. Our time is very flexible, so it's easy for us to rearrange our schedule.

Do you have any weekday morning rituals? — *Hung-Ming:* In the morning, after taking our daughter to school, I usually go back home to have a coffee and check emails with Chen-Yen. Then we go to our studio—sometimes I bike if the weather is nice. Before going up to the studio, we usually like to spend an hour at Konstfack library to find inspiration.

Who do you admire creatively? — *Chen-Yen:* Yohji Yamamoto. I see him as a coexistence of art and design with a distinctive sophistication. He's very unique and upholds his theory in his mind and practice way beyond ordinary thinking. I always wonder how determined and talented he must be to live this way. *Hung-Ming:* I like Greta Grossman. Her work is simple with unique character. One of my favorite designs of hers is the Grossman desk: It's more like a beautiful sculpture than a piece of furniture.

What was the process of starting your company, Afteroom? — *Hung-Ming:* We started Afteroom in the middle of 2011. In the beginning, we wanted to produce products by ourselves, so we contacted our favorite tea farms, bicycle companies and clothing factories to make our products. *Chen-Yen:* It was scary and fun at the same time, but we knew we needed to give our idea a try, so we just did it without hesitation.

How did you choose the name Afteroom? — *Chen-Yen:* We value the relationship between time and space, so we created the word *Afteroom*, which means the transformation a space experiences over a long period of time.

Please tell us a bit more about your company's values. — *Chen-Yen:* "Advocate of the traces of time" is the main idea behind Afteroom, and all of our designs embody the spirit of it. We simply want to create things people won't get rid of—something you'd like to keep for now and also leave for the next generation. Only purity can last for a long time. Life is short and we have to fulfill what we really want to do, and this concept matches our personalities deeply. We just don't like to waste our lives creating something that's contrary to who we are. While we're working, we try to follow our hearts.

What do you each bring to the creative process? — *Hung-Ming:* We discuss ideas together, then I do the sketches from our ideas and make the 3-D models. Chen-Yen takes charge of the overall image, including the proportion and colors, and she chooses which projects should continue and which should stop. I've been trained as an industrial and interior designer for a long time, so I know how to operate CAD software and the mass-production process. However, I get blinded easily, so Chen-Yen takes on the great responsibility of director. She has a good eye to judge whether something is good or bad and isn't afraid to hurt my feelings.

What's your philosophy regarding the durability of an object, both aesthetically and practically? — *Hung-Ming:* One day I looked at our daughter and was surprised by how quickly she'd been growing. In that moment, I realized that she's our ruler of time: The taller she is, the older we are. The fact is that there will be a day when we leave her. Maybe that's part of the reason we decided to make furniture; our furniture can replace us by staying with her. When we're gone, she can still feel our presence by using our chairs or sofa. Maybe one day she can go abroad and see other people sitting on our chairs and proudly say, "Hey! That's my parents' chair!" On the other hand, she might also feel fed up with our furniture and want to get rid of it! You never know.

Hung-Ming, how did your experience working as a technology designer shape your current design philosophy with Afteroom? — *Hung-Ming:* While I was working in a company that produced consumer electronics, I learned that lots of electronic gadgets end up in the trash within a few years, mainly because new technology keeps evolving with super-high speed. Even though there's nothing wrong with new technology, it's scary for a designer that a phone or keyboard you design may only survive two years and you'll never see it again. Now I'm happy to focus on interior and furniture designs that have a much longer life span than new technology.

Chen-Yen, how has your background in fashion influenced your work with Afteroom? — *Chen-Yen:* While working as an assistant fashion designer, I learned to process the details of ongoing projects quickly, racing against time day after day. Experiencing this in my early 20s deeply improved my sensitivity to color combinations and taught me how to internalize aesthetics. Both help while I'm working: The sensory intuition and aesthetic judgment I obtained determines the direction of our studio. Just like Hung-Ming, I love things that will last for a lifetime. This was the concept we started our company with, and it's totally different from fashion. Sometimes you just need to go around in a circle to find your true self.

WORDS
RACHEL EVA LIM

MEMORY LANE

Our memories play an instrumental role in preserving our personal and family narratives. While older generations fostered these stories by developing photographs, writing letters and composing ballads, we're more likely to do so using digital photo-sharing platforms. Perhaps it's time to consider how we're building our family archives for the future.

Memories are one of the most important components of establishing our identities. Throughout our lives, we engage in a constant cycle of building, shaping and cultivating our personal histories through these snippets of moments passed, adding and subtracting stories that preserve the narratives we hold most dear. These memories remind us of who we are and where we've been—they're living, breathing entities stored in our brains that we intimately interact with on a daily basis.

In the past, narratives were often passed down through generations and reinforced in the form of oral histories, ballads, songs, folklore, diaries and handwritten letters. The amount of time and careful attention spent crafting these relics and partaking in these rituals gave them a sense of meaning, significance and sacredness.

Although photography has been a prominent documentation tool since the 1920s, the rapid growth in popularity of disposable cameras in the 1980s positioned photography as the dominant way we record our personal and family histories. Relatively inexpensive and easy to carry around, these handy contraptions allowed users to develop their snapshots into objects that could be easily slotted into a family album. These memories—once only an intangible series of firing synapses—

Despite the volume of pictures we're taking, our ability to reminisce and strengthen the stories they tell is negated if we don't carve out the time to actually look at them.

were suddenly given an instantly gratifying physical form. Thanks to these affordable cameras, photographs overtook rambling verbal odysseys and inherited ephemera to become the predominant way of documenting special moments in our lives. They gave us the ability to pause time and allow our future selves to look back on a life well lived among the people we love.

Families would unearth these albums after anniversary dinners or holiday parties and use the images as a launching point to recount stories about everything from summers spent at Lake George to that one time you accidentally singed off your little sister's eyebrows with a curling iron. Gathering around this tangible object filled with meaning gave families the opportunity to look back at their collective past through a collection of key moments amassed over the years. These photographs brought them together to share communal stories, equipping their children with a ready supply of (often embarrassing) narratives to begin constructing their own sense of self.

Photography continues to be one of the primary ways we create family narratives today, but changes in technology have drastically altered both how we go about capturing these moments and the way we interact with them after the shutter has clicked. The widespread availability of smartphones and digital cameras has greatly increased the number of photographs we can take and the ease with which we can take them, and we're less likely to spend evenings huddled around a leather-bound book revisiting our own images than we are double tapping others' on our lunch breaks. The family album has been demoted to the dusty attic, instead replaced by Instagram feeds and status updates.

How has this changed the way we construct our personal histories, and what does it mean for the concept of family going forward? While convenience certainly has its upside, our changing relationship with technology has had a fundamental impact on how we visually record our experiences, share them with others and go about weaving these photographs into the central fabric of our personal narratives.

Family stories are crucial to building our sense of belonging within immediate circles while also informing our individual identities. We put immense stock in the stories we're told from childhood, and we use these tales to construct a narrative that helps shape our understanding of who we are and the history of the family we come from. These familial fables also work to help us understand our context in the greater world and position ourselves within our communities.

"Family stories have all sorts of functions, but one of them is that they provide a set of instructions for interacting with the world," says Dr. Elizabeth Stone, a writer and English professor at Fordham University, who has written extensively about how family stories play an instrumental role in shaping identity. Aside from making us feel connected to our heritage, perhaps the most important aspect of these narratives is how they provide the context and foundation to help us define ourselves as individuals. "Family stories seem to persist in importance even when people think of themselves individually, without regard to their familial roles," she writes in her book, *Black Sheep and Kissing Cousins: How Our Family Stories Shape Us*. "The particular human chain we're part of is central to our individual identity. Even if we loathe

We're now less likely to spend evenings huddled around a leather-bound photo album revisiting our own images than we are double tapping others' on our lunch breaks.

our families, in order to know ourselves, we seem to need to know about them, just as prologue."

That's because we're not bound by the stories of our past, and we always have the chance to forge a new future off the foundation that we inherit. As we grow older, move away from our original kin and begin to form our own, our family histories continue to matter, but sometimes in new ways. "At moments of major life transitions, we may claim certain of our stories, take them over, shape them, reshape them and put our own stamp on them," Stone says. "We make them part of us instead of making ourselves part of them."

We use photography as a tool to document these important episodes in our lives—by clicking a button, we create noteworthy moments that we'll keep revisiting for years. Dr. Linda Henkel is a professor of psychology at Fairfield University who has conducted numerous studies on the relationship between photography and memory. She likens selecting what we want to capture to choosing which moments we want to preserve in our memories, thereby deciding the course of our personal narratives. "When we look at photos—like those of our childhood, for example— we're selectively shaping what's accessible," Henkel says. "The stories we tell and the photos we choose to look at absolutely shape our memories." As Winston Churchill once said, "History is written by the victors."

Deciding to only photograph certain slivers of our experiences inevitably leaves out the millions more that don't make it into our mental collections. The stories that have been omitted matter just as much to the construction of our histories as those

that were captured as the photographs we take and choose to look back on determine the memories that become blurry and those we constantly sharpen. By being more conscientious of the snapshots we take on a daily basis, we can influence the way we reflect on and remember our experiences— influencing our personal histories and the narratives our families will continue to tell years down the road.

Photography's technological advances have changed the way we use the medium as a mechanism for both documentation and memory retrieval. While storytelling, letter writing and journal writing are still used to record the experiences we want to remember, the accessibility and convenience of both photo-taking devices and photo-sharing platforms have made photography the dominant medium we use to document our lives. We've been quick to adopt and adapt to these new devices, enjoying the ease with which we can create, preserve and share our family experiences by simply pulling a smartphone out of our back pockets and swiping at a screen.

Until recently, the cost of film and the extra step of needing to develop our photographs limited the number of pictures we took. Our Victorian-era ancestors, who stood on the cusp of photography's late-19th-century boom, reserved taking pictures for official family portraits and important ceremonies. The price and time investment of this venture ensured that they only recorded salient experiences that were truly important to them—moments that they wanted preserved for years to come. "Celluloid images were relatively limited and expensive, so they'd have to make conscious decisions about what they chose to capture and what they thought that moment meant at the point of capture," says Dr. David White, head of technology-enhanced learning at the University of the Arts London. After spending much of his time investigating the dynamics of digital distribution, he stresses that the ease with which we snap pictures these days has dramatically changed our approach to photography and its effect on memory.

"[The time and effort it once took to take a photograph] would help to cement the moment in our memories and actually amplify our recall of the moment," he says. "Now we can capture an unlimited number of images and don't curate in the moment. The result is we have hundreds of images of an event, but we're less emotionally attached to them. They contain less meaning, because we didn't have to think about what they represented when we took them."

The widespread availability of image-recording gadgets has led to a shift in the function of instant photography. Instead of using a camera to document personal histories for our family members to reflect on in the future, we're now able to harness it as a public communication device to connect us with online communities instantly. "People aren't necessarily taking photos anymore for the purpose of documenting their experiences and being able to have a memory cue to use later on," Henkel says. "So many people now take photographs because they want to communicate in the moment—they want to show other people what they're doing, where they are and how they're feeling."

Photographs are no longer just mementos to use as memory cues that prompt future discussions about our most treasured tales. Instead, we're more likely to use our cameras to broadcast our in-the-moment experiences for immediate gratification.

This has given an entirely new meaning to the family album. In addition to thinking less about the future significance of the photographs we're taking, we're also increasingly using public social-media platforms to project our family stories. In the past, our photographs rarely made it outside our homes, but now we readily share intimate and often embarrassing images with near-strangers, from naked baby snapshots to evidence of our mortifying journeys through puberty. Facebook and Instagram have taken the place of the traditional family album by transporting our images out of the living room and onto the internet. Instead of keeping the most precious moments of our lives private—for our families and loved ones alone—we're sharing these items of immense value with our online communities. And that has its consequences.

"I think of the public or semipublic digital sphere as the 'front parlor' of our lives—the place where we 'perform' the best version of ourselves," White says. "We curate what we imagine will reflect the aspects of our lives with the highest social capital. The private family album contained elements of this, but it was less performative. It was a more humble recording of the passage of time and significant events."

Courtney Adamo, cofounder of the Babyccino Kids website and a mother of four, often grapples with this notion. She has more than 100,000 followers on Instagram and posts a variety of snapshots of her family online, ranging from road trips and days at the beach to candid portraits of her kids at home. "I'm sure that knowing my photographs are public has shaped the way I document my family life, as it's like opening up a photo album or scrapbook to hundreds and thousands of strangers," Adamo says. "But I don't usually document the overly personal or intimate details on Instagram. I reserve these images for a private blog that only my close family sees and reads."

Depending on the way we approach sharing our personal photographs online, there are both benefits and drawbacks of using these platforms as both storytelling devices and virtual storage systems for our memories. "Our online networks tend toward homophily [the tendency of individuals to associate and bond with people who are similar to them]. What we share is a narrow-minded performance of what we feel others in our group will be impressed with," White says. "We can be tempted to curate a very particular version of our lives, and that can be tiring to maintain or may leave us feeling hollow and without meaningful human connection." But White also insists that it's not all doom and gloom, as our virtual networks can also expose us to a plethora of different lifestyles that give us new insight into our own. "On the plus side, the wider web can make the rich variation of the many different ways of living visible, highlighting that there's more than one way to be successful or happy," he adds.

Hideaki Hamada is a Japanese photographer who publishes an ongoing series of photographs of his two young sons, Haru and Mina, on various online platforms as well as in galleries and books. "Shooting them gives me this strange feeling that I'm watching myself reliving my own life," Hamada says. "It's given me a chance to reflect on my own identity and to view the world from a different perspective. I've found parts of myself that I'd never known before, which has had a huge impact on shaping my sense of self today."

Hamada's project gives him an opportunity to spend lots of quality time with his sons, but he also hopes it will encourage his viewers to spend more time with their own families and share their own stories. "While I definitely compile albums that are just for my family, I wanted this series to be something that's both social and public in nature," he says. "When people look at my images, it would be nice if they began to recall their own past."

Unfortunately though, it seems that we're starting to rely on our smartphones and digital cameras instead of committing our experiences to memory. In one of Henkel's experiments, she instructed her subjects to walk around the Bellarmine Museum of Art in Connecticut. Half of them were told to take photographs of certain objects while the others actively observed their surroundings. "What I found was that, when they came back a day or two later and I asked them to remember what had been part of the tour, the students taking photographs remembered fewer of the objects and fewer details about them than those who had simply observed in the moment," Henkel says. "Taking the photo actually harmed memory."

Henkel believes that the individuals who took photographs of the objects were outsourcing their memories to their cameras and counted on these devices to remember the experience for them. Instead of using their full cognitive function to pay attention and generate a memory of their surroundings, the camera presented an opportunity for them to refrain from expending that energy.

However, Henkel is quick to stress that depending on cameras and other devices to capture our memories may not necessarily be a bad thing: What really affects the quality of the memories we're creating is our interaction with the photographs once they've been taken. "It's not a bad strategy, right? If the camera captures it for us, then we can use our cognitive resources to be engaged with other kinds of things," she says. "Except the problem is that we take so many photos that we don't have the time to look through them." The switch to digital photography has allowed us to accumulate more pictures of our families and loved ones than ever before. But despite the volume and variety of pictures we're taking, our ability to reminisce and strengthen the stories they tell is negated if we don't carve out time to actually look at them.

Gathering around printed images—such as those we keep in a family photo album—has a significant impact on how we and our families recall memories and craft stories around them. When we take the time to pause and look back on the photographs we've taken, especially in the presence of others, we give ourselves an opportunity to engage in communal dialogue about our experiences. If we don't set aside time for these interactions, we limit our recall to solo fleeting visual encounters that mostly happen when organizing our online photo libraries or clearing out our memory cards. "Images are simply a proxy for memory, not the memory itself,"

Although being discriminating about what images to capture may require more thought and energy at the time, it allows us to curate the family albums of the future.

White says. Henkel agrees with this sentiment: "A photo isn't going to be useful as a memory cue if you don't take the time to look at it," she adds.

Although many of us possess impressive collections of digital family snapshots, they're basically useless for reinforcing our identities if we don't revisit them and use them to spark thoughtful conversations about the past. When combined with face-to-face banter, these images provoke a genuine community connection that's greater than the sum of the pixels' parts. "It's that sort of reminiscing that really brings the photos to life and helps preserve the memories," Henkel says.

Another method for connecting more with both the present moment and the future memories we're inevitably creating is to approach the act of taking photographs with a more discerning and thoughtful eye. One of the obstacles to revisiting our image libraries is the sheer overwhelming number of digital snapshots we need to wade through to get to the ones that truly matter. "I love photographs and think that they're absolutely useful as memory cues," Henkel says, "but we could be more selective about the photos we're taking." Although being discriminating about what images to capture may require more thought and energy at the time of creation, it allows us to curate the family albums of the future by being more selective about what we're snapping in the moment.

And while some may balk at the additional steps required to print out digital snapshots and store them properly, the experience of holding a tangible photo album in our hands and flipping through it with our favorite people dramatically changes our interaction with the both our family and the images themselves. The mere act of turning the pages encourages us to slow down, spend a few more minutes dwelling on the memories that each image evokes and trading anecdotes rather than hastily scrolling through someone's digital album or social-media feed. Henkel herself is an advocate for this method of preservation.

"I'm a little bit old-school," she says. "My grandson, Evan, is 10 months old now. I've printed out two albums of him with about 500 photos in them. I'm not going to sit down and go through the thousands of photos I've taken of him on the computer, but when I print them out and bring the book to my father to show him his great-grandson, I find that very satisfying," she says. "Nowadays people pass around a phone, and the way you swipe through them feels less meaningful. Looking at physical photo albums sort of has more weight to it."

The evolving nature of photography provides us with an invaluable medium to document our experiences, effectively presenting us with new ways of framing and creating our family stories. But while the immense popularity of public photo-sharing platforms shows no signs of stopping any time soon, bringing a more thoughtful approach to our relationship with the photographs we take can enrich both our family narratives and our connections with our loved ones as a whole. By fully immersing ourselves in our present experiences and taking the time to revisit our photographs and remember the past, we're creating family histories that we can grow old with for years to come and be proud to pass on to future generations.

WORDS
STEPHANIE ROSENBAUM KLASSEN

PHOTOGRAPHS
NEIL BEDFORD

STYLING
RACHEL CAULFIELD

Are We There Yet?

Road trips are all about freedom, adventure and new perspectives, with a bit of nostalgia and fried food thrown in. Although we can now look up the answer to a trivia question rather than feuding about it for 35 miles, stowing away the screens and staring out the window can take us back to simpler times and deeper conversations.

What is it about the magic of the open road? Is it the lure of the unknown, the highway's yellow Morse code unspooling in the distance like Dorothy's way to Oz? Is it the promise of exploring places we've never been, of lighting out for the territories and leaving our everyday selves behind? Or is it the joy of following a well-trodden path, of reassuring ourselves that this once-loved general store, goofy road sign or gnarled apple orchard has continued on, same as ever, waiting patiently for our return?

We travel for discovery, to find new experiences or to measure our growth against the ever-evolving landscape of the decades. But the journey comes before the destination and for many of us, the family road trip was our first foray into that wider unknown world.

Oh, the memories! Of carsickness and sing-alongs, of forgotten Hershey's bars melted between the seats, of leaving pajama-clad in the predawn hours, of learning to hold our breath every time a cemetery passed outside the window. We pleaded for ice cream whenever the red roof of a Dairy Queen was spotted in the distance—idiosyncratic landmarks such as these were guideposts along the highway more than the mileposts.

Back then, food was different on the road. Seagulls swooped in to steal French fries dropped under the picnic table. Sandwiches, just a little squashed but still tasting of home, were doled out from an Igloo cooler at a highway rest stop. Date-shake stands dotted the highways of the Southern California desert. Czech pastries punctuated the flat prairie roads of Nebraska.

Time seemed to pass differently on the road—as elastic as salt water taffy. Stuck in the backseat for hours on end, we had to rely on each other for fun. The laws requiring kids' car seats have made some old-school diversions obsolete—like taking turns to crawl from the backseat into Dad's lap to throw change into the turnpike's toll baskets—but many tried-and-true road-trip games remain.

These games may change from generation to generation and from country to country, but we all have fond (or not so fond, depending on how much sibling pinching was involved) memories of how we once giggled, whined or suffered through our time in the station wagon or minivan. What American child hasn't played the license plate game, searching for different states' plates as if the road was one huge atlas? Some played "Spotto," pointing out each rare passing yellow car. And whether you called it "Punch Buggy!" or "Slug Bug!," many of us probably started backseat warfare every time a Volkswagen Beetle was spied on the road. Then there are the classics such as 20 Questions, I-Spy or the memory-mangling picnic game, many of which are worth reviving among the adults once off the road, perhaps while passing around a fine bottle of whiskey.

The boxy Volvos and the lumbering Buicks of yesteryear may have ceded to sleeker hybrids and SUVs, but the serendipitous joys of family time on the road can still be replicated. The trick is stowing the electronic devices for the duration, replacing the diversion of Snapchat and the umpteenth showing of *Frozen* with stories, songs and roadside entertainment. Temporarily unplugging from technology can be challenging, but it allows us to stare out the window and pay closer attention to unexpected sights. Is there a petrified forest asking for exploration? The world's largest collection of salt and pepper shakers begging to be seen? How about popping into an alligator farm or a mermaid show? Road trips call for embracing the odd and unknown, making friends with every diner waiter along the way and spitting watermelon seeds out the windows. Rest assured, fights will happen. But the shared moments of triumph are what we'll remember: The rocks flawlessly skipped across a nameless river, the indigo grins from a still-warm slice of blueberry pie and the sudden, blissful quiet that comes while zooming though an old mountainside train tunnel.

A family travels together, for better or worse, through time as well as space. And the family that sings off-key on their quest for the best fish-and-chips in Ireland or bison burgers in Montana is one that will always have stories to tell, no matter how many years and miles come to pass.

PHOTOGRAPHS
MAJA DANIELS

Twin

Set

*Monette and Mady aren't just identical—they're inseparable.
The Parisian twins live in the same apartment, dress alike, dance
together and share every meal. Swedish photographer Maja Daniels
has spent a great deal of time documenting their everyday lives.*

What childhood memories do you cherish the most?

Mady: I think it must be going on vacation with our parents. We used to visit our grandparents in the mountains in the Auvergne region in central France. We loved going there.

Monette: I have memories: visions of the sky and the mountains and a strong feeling of freedom. We used to go hiking high up the mountains with our father. He loved hiking—we would walk for miles on end.

Mady: That's where we learned to use our legs! We often danced together in the small square in the village. We loved dancing together.

Monette: We never miss the occasion to dance, whether it's at a party or just simply because we feel like it.

You're both professional dancers. How does being so intimate help your dancing? Are you more in tune with each other?

Monette: When you're dancing with somebody, you become a new couple. You have to spend time with someone and be able to share in order to make it work.

Mady: Therefore it's easier for us to dance together since we already know and understand each other so well. Because we're in the habit of being close, extending this unity into dancing was easy.

What has your close bond taught you about the notion of family?

Mady: Our close relationship helps us deal better with all sorts of other relationships. The foundation you receive from your family is important, and it helps us evolve within other families in life.

Monette: Thanks to our relationship as twins, it's very easy for us to integrate into other groups.

Mady: I think we understand more about being a couple than most individuals do.

Have you ever wished that you were an only child?

Monette: But why?

Mady: Oh, no, never! It's not important for us to have differences. No, it's just in our nature.

Monette: We're very happy together. We've never had such a wish. You can be on your own even if you're with someone.

Please tell us what you've learned about communication.

Mady: Our communication with each other is very specific and something quite special. It's simple. We can say things to each other that we wouldn't say to others—even if it hurts, we can say it. It's more honest.

Monette: And we can communicate without talking. Our brains are wired to function together.

Mady: Earlier today we were doing two things at the same time without talking about them—we just knew what was going on.

Do you have different roles when it comes to organizing your lives?

Monette: Ultimately, and this is true for all aspects of life, we fill certain roles in order to find unity. And in order to find this unity, the role must be understood by both parts. When dancing together, for an example, you have to be 50–50, not 40–60.

Mady: Each person has to take his or her responsibility, and this sharing is easy for us. Twins have a better sense of sharing. A single child doesn't like to share, but a twin will share, because they consider themselves a unit already. Without us knowing, this sharing is already integrated in our brains. So I won't enter into Monette's space and she won't enter into mine, naturally.

Monette: It's a kind of mutual respect.

Mady: There's a lyricism when sharing is done well. It's quite magical. It's a unity that goes beyond a "me-you" type of sharing. The trick is to not notice this 50–50 split.

Neither of you has ever been married. What similarities and differences do you share with married couples?

Mady: It's two different types of couples! A married couple has only known each other for a short amount of time. The important thing to point out here is that they weren't born together, even if they've been together for 60 years.

What's the most special thing about your relationship?

Mady: Our bond. This is the most important thing for a twin. There is this invisible bond between us.

Monette: Oh yes, it's the key! It's really the sixth sense for a twin, because it's there even before birth. We can feel it. I'm not sure our mother liked it too much in the beginning—she used to question our identical outfits. But ultimately, she came around.

Mady: But it's difficult to describe, because it's something mysterious. It's beyond words or gesticulations or looks. Psychologists say the ultimate difference is that we've shared placenta—it's as simple as that.

Monette: It's a kind of communication between us. And it's because of this bond that there's harmony between us.

Mady: Also, another special aspect to our relationship is that it's honest—we can't lie to each other.

Monette: Yes, and we don't need to speak to each other all the time. Each person can pick up on what the other one is feeling, so we don't need to state obvious things.

Mady: We understand each other.

Monette: We know each other!

What else has your relationship taught you?

Monette: It has taught us a lot about compromise, of course.

Mady: There are always compromises to be made; our lives are made of them. But that doesn't mean we're better at it than others.

What's the most important lesson that your sister has taught you?

Monette: To Love.

Mady: Yes, exactly. But Love with a big L, of course! I'm not talking about romance.

Monette: We're always there for each other. If there's something to share, we share it.

Mady: If something difficult happens to one of us, the other one is there. All of the small things are important; the little nothings.

Monette: That's Love.

These images were shot by Maja Daniels, a Swedish photographer based in London. When Maja first spotted Mady and Monette on the streets of Paris, she was immediately captivated by their identical outfits, synchronized mannerisms and quirky demeanor. She began photographing both posed portraits and documentary images of their everyday lives. Maja approaches her projects through a sociological frame and is interested in issues related to self-identity. She believes encountering the twins' unique bond makes us wonder, "Is that the same person twice?"

TO SEE MORE IMAGES OF MONETTE AND MADY, PLEASE VISIT MAJADANIELS.COM

ILLUSTRATIONS
KATRIN COETZER

Bridging
the Distance

When we're old enough to decide where to set down our roots, some of us choose to cross countries and seas whereas others elect not to fall far from the family tree. We ask three writers to consider the benefits and drawbacks of living close to your relatives, far away from them and how to form your own version of family no matter where you are.

WORDS
DAISY HILDYARD

NEAR

With every home-cooked meal comes a barrage of unsolicited opinions: Sharing a house with your family or even just living around the corner from them has its ups and downs.

Family can be more like a force of nature than something we choose. After all, even the closest connection is no guarantee that your relatives are relatively like you at all. As we grow older, many people make up for this preordained allocation by opting to put an ocean between themselves and their childhood bedrooms, but some of us retain an instinctive desire to endure living near our kin. For those who do, there are many benefits that these relationships foster.

Plenty of reasons exist for why we might choose to return to our family homes in our later years: We may face financial adversity (thanks, student loans), come back to look after an older relative or simply have a deep-seated affinity for our hometown's deep-dish pizza. Whether we've recently returned from an adventure abroad or never actually left the nest, there is a calm yet chaotic nostalgia that comes with sharing oxygen with your parents once more.

Whether you cohabit in a house, a neighborhood or a city, many of us hope that living near our family will return us to a simpler life. And in some ways, it does: It can help us edit unnecessary baggage from our lives and devote that newfound time to personal projects. There are also practical benefits: There's no need to worry about holiday traffic. You can eat your dad's cooking twice a week. Small luxuries such as child care, free rides to the airport and extra hands when moving house are available on request.

But sharing a physical space may also encroach on your mental space. Being in close proximity to your family means that your loved ones are inherently implicated in your daily life. Whether you cross paths with them at your local supermarket or in the hallway, someone will always have something to say about the choices you're making, be it about the granola you're buying or the shoes you're wearing. They'll share their opinions on anything you care to discuss, along with a few things you don't care to discuss at all. They'll offer sentiments on posture, gender, the international panel on climate change, how to chop an onion and the local public transportation system. And as frustrating as it may be, you have to remember that your grandmother has lived through wars and revolutions, careers and husbands, so she's earned the right to make impolite noises about your impractical clothing or your weirdly named kids.

Living near family can be supportive and grounding, but it also forces you to confront your origins. The only way to prevent your kin's ever-present opinions from overwhelming you is to speak your mind when you really need to, and to let it go when you don't. Avoiding conflict and enjoying a fight are both skills, but they require paying attention to your relatives' changing moods and minds. Sometimes, every relative needs their own room—both mentally and literally.

WORDS
KELSEY SNELL

FAR

Although putting space between ourselves and our families can teach us independence, it's perfectly normal to admit that you sometimes still need them.

Leaving home and loving home don't have to be at odds with one another. Despite what our grandmothers' rib-cracking hugs lead us to believe, our families never intended to keep us—only to make and teach us, and to love us enough to let us go.

Enter distance; she complicates everything and yet sweetens the pot. It's not in spite of home but because of it that we're miles, time zones and oceans away—hungry for adventure and out to find our own. Psychologist John Bowlby's attachment theory suggests it's key in a child's development to have a "secure base," such as a parent they trust who will be there when they return from exploring. Because of this reliable base, independence begins to take shape. We eventually fling ourselves from the coop, swerving solo and headlong into chaotic midtown streets, standoffish living situations, cultures of every strata and overpriced, under-lit bars in the name of "finding ourselves."

But some days you just need a back-scratch more than a happy hour. Far from home, we miss its ease and unsolicited affections, the little tender moments and the Wednesday minutiae. We miss being known. And when one thing triggers the homesickness, it all falls down. Add a little heartbreak to your miserable morning commute and that unspoken plea of "come home" on the end of the line can suddenly begin to sound like the best solution—even when it's not.

This is because our secure base is our people, not a location. Those relationships can stand firm among the zigzagging, sling-shotting trajectory of our nomadic lives. But if we miss a call, the next and another, we can't let remorse prevent us from picking up the phone to return it, or let guilt make us lazy. And as unnatural and awkward as a video chat feels, there are few better options to make someone feel immediately connected. While we yearn for an all-elusive handwritten note, letters lack the spontaneity of tech—sometimes a surprise FaceTime high five is what your sister needs right before her last college exam.

That said, our inability to deliver that perfect grandiose gesture shouldn't prevent us from letting our families into our everyday lives. Jotting an inside joke on a postcard, leaving an "I love you" message as your train makes an overground appearance or emailing a photo and the menu from last night's dinner with girlfriends can make them feel just as—if not more than—connected.

But sometimes, going home really is the answer. There's no place like home to bring a weary soul, a victory or a no-frills persona needing little more than a bowl of cereal and a hug. When we hop in the car or buy that plane ticket, we're not admitting defeat—only that we're tired. After putting up with the bitter exhaustion of the unknown, we can now taste the sweetness of coming home.

WORDS
LIZ CLAYTON

WHEREVER YOU ARE

Your current family situation doesn't have to dictate your future one: Finding your own meaning of family can reinforce your relationships with all parties involved.

It happens. By chance or by choice, you've suddenly found yourself a grown-up, either far from home, far from family or without a family to be far from. Whether we're building or rebuilding one, the families we choose are part of the places where we put down roots—the building blocks aiming into the skies of our future selves.

The idea of choosing our own families may first come out of necessity: They spring from that need for comfort, support and Thanksgiving tablemates that appear when you're a fish out of kindred water. But what starts as a provisional measure reveals itself to be a deeper statement. That community of friends that becomes your local family—from the accidental buddies at the gym

and laundromat to romantic partners that you've sought out with more intention—is a radiating circle of who you truly are today. They reflect your realized (or realizing) adult self, a person whose goals and interests are informed—but not defined—by who you were in college, who you are among your siblings or who you'll become in later chapters of your life.

Of course, there's a nuance lost in these new families: They aren't able to post embarrassing throwback photos of you online or remind you of the time your sweet station wagon with the eight-track player blew up downtown while you were ditching high school. But what they do bring is an optimism, a clean slate and the

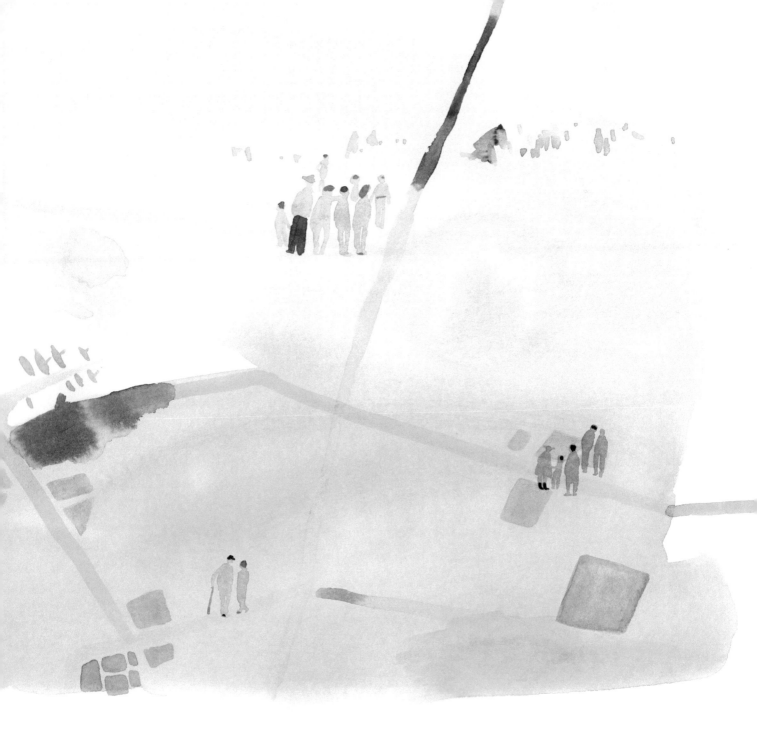

welcoming arms of those who also seek a sense of closeness that, in many ways, is harder to build from the ground up.

You can learn a lot about yourself through the families you fall into in a new environment. Whether it's the married couple who always has a place at the table for you, the neighbor who brings you freshly cut flowers or the teenager in the corner store you always buy a candy bar for, how you nurture and let yourself be nurtured—and by who—can reveal what you want from intimacy. While our birth families, bless them, are preselected for us (warts and all), our friend families allow us to choose different warts that may be more compatible with our own—or that will teach us more about them.

For those lucky enough to have both kinds of kin, there's a sweet space between the comfort of those who've always known you and understand precisely how you work and the tabula rasa of those you've newly drawn near. We're all products of both our past and present selves and all the little stages in between. We're able to find our true selves in that harmony, gathering what and who we choose to make us strong and loving and making this new world our own.

And if we should fear that we're cheating on the families we came from? Without a doubt, they want this world for you, a place where you'll thrive and where the kitchen table is never empty.

WORDS
ANNU SUBRAMANIAN

PHOTOGRAPHS
BERTIL NILSSON

STYLING
ROSE FORDE

Lean on Me

Respect, admiration and trust: These are some of the qualities that we look for in our compatriots. The spark that ignites when two people bond can be both unexpected and exhilarating.

If only we could collect and bottle the power of those rare moments of true bonding. An electric current runs through them, crackling with unfettered conversation, glowing with shared warmth. When we bond with someone else, we surrender our desire for power and our need to know the next chess move. The reason two people come together is rarely why they stay close, but it does offer an entry point. Unlikely allies are formed against common enemies. Bicoastal night owls reconnect online as an insomnia antidote. New residents in a foreign city travel together. In life, we often first connect with someone in response to something outside ourselves, but the relationship only grows as we let in more personal aspects of our lives. It's thrilling to confess to something and be received with wide-eyed understanding or an incredulous *me too*! Sometimes this happens in slow motion as we come to care for each other over several conversations. Other times, connections are sparked instantly, such as a dry quip muttered to another person in the waiting room that snowballs into a tête-à-tête of jokes. The author Vivian Gornick describes those moments when strangers brush up against one another and share an unexpected connection as "the drama of human beings sighting each other across the isolation." In other words, we bond because our chaos sees theirs. Realizing that need to be received is imperative to both old and new bonds. They necessitate presence—an imaginary circle drawn around two people and what exists within it. We match each other's intonation and pace, we point our toes in a partner's direction, we tilt our heads in the same way, we hide our hands in our faces while laughing until giving in to full-bellied bellows. That space we share feels suspended from the activities and insecurities that usually distract us. But sometimes we don't realize the beauty in these moments until much later—we were too absorbed in each other's eccentricities to notice. Now, that's intimacy.

COMMENSALITY:

THE ART OF EATING TOGETHER

_____

The word commensality *refers to the practice of coming together around
a table to break both bread and boundaries. It comes from the Latin*
commensalis, *which combines the terms* com *("together") and* mensa
*("table"). Until now, the word has been mostly confined to textbooks and
academia, but we believe it should be brought into everyday use.
After all, eating together is one of the few social conventions that everyone
takes part in, regardless of our backgrounds. We interview two of the editors of*
Commensality: From Everyday Food to Feast *to help us learn more.*

In their book, *Commensality: From Everyday Food to Feast* (Bloomsbury, 2015), editors Susanne Kerner, Cynthia Chou and Morten Warmind—all professors at the University of Copenhagen, Denmark—consider the ways that human beings have eaten together in different cultures and eras. Since most of us more commonly experience commensality around a dinner or breakfast table, they didn't just focus on the fancy feasts and big banquets of times passed, but instead highlighted the traditions and rituals that surround the average daily meal. Incorporating insight from anthropologists, historians and archaeologists, the book digs deeply into the social benefits of sharing meals. Here, two of the book's editors weigh in on what commensality is and why it's important in bringing us all together.

WHY IS COMMENSALITY ESSENTIAL FOR SOCIETY?
Morten: Eating is one of the few absolute necessities. To eat in the company of others is a strong expression of trust and "togetherness" of a much higher order than just "being together." It's this kind of togetherness that societies are made of, and therefore commensality is essential for them. Eating requires preparation and violence: Chewing is a kind of violence, even if what we chew is dead or a vegetable. Plants are alive and require killing too—death is a harvester. So the act of eating is indispensable and delicate and vulnerable, all at the same time. We don't have to eat together every day and all the time, but that trust has to be reaffirmed regularly.
Susanne: Eating together certainly helps to create, strengthen and renegotiate the social relations and

bonds between people in a group, such as a family. Eating and drinking together plays a large role in organizing a society today—such as who invites whom, who sits next to whom—and it played an equally large role in the past, when commensality was the practice for negotiating social relations and hierarchies. Hierarchy, heterarchy, closeness of relations and power relations are all expressed in commensality—and that applies to family dinners as much as formal dinners for foreign heads of state.

WHY IS IT IMPORTANT THAT FAMILIES COME TOGETHER FOR MEALS? WHAT ISSUES COME FROM EATING ALONE?

Morten: If we eat on our own when we feel like it—which I'm sure we're actually more comfortable doing—we're expressing a strong distrust of society. If family members don't regularly eat together, they're basically declaring the family to be a common name and address, nothing more. It should be noted that for commensality to exist, there must be equal access to all foods. The reason we have societies is so that we can be better together than any individual member can be alone. So having a simple inclusive discussion of everything, which can be part of eating together, will improve everyone's ability to make points and understand them.

WHAT ARE SOME OF THE PROBLEMS THAT ARISE OVER TIME WHEN FAMILIES DON'T EAT REGULAR MEALS TOGETHER?

Morten: They'll start to regard each other as instruments or obstacles and not as equal members of a group. They demonstrate a mistrust or indifference that they actually may not feel, and the togetherness of the family will disintegrate. Sometimes the only thing that keeps them held together is the thought of the economic and practical difficulties that would follow if the family were to dissolve, but the net of emotional ties between family members can be so strong that it makes up for the lack of group identity. Families may find other ways than eating together to express togetherness, but none is quite so strong.

Susanne: If the relations in a family are not all right, eating together will not help. The opposite may happen, making eating together very uncomfortable. On the other hand, eating together—which is a normal routine in a country like France—leads to less obesity than when all family members eat alone.

IN WHAT WAYS DOES COMMENSALITY IMPACT OUR EMOTIONAL AND PHYSICAL HEALTH?

Morten: Because eating is a time of vulnerability, we're often more comfortable eating on our own. But it's unhealthy for us to do so—emotionally as well as physically, because we constantly need to practice our social skills and experience the enjoyment of being with other people and performing "togetherness." Some people have so much trouble doing this that it could be regarded as an emotional disorder.

WHAT DOES THE TERM *FAMILY* MEAN TO YOU?

Morten: I don't like the idea of "blood relatives" as a concept. Families are based on unions of people who aren't specifically blood relatives.

Susanne: I agree that families being made up of blood relatives is a rather strange concept, as it excludes stepmothers, adopted children, a husband and wife alone, etc. We should ignore that and define family in the sense of a small group of people living together—for example, a group of youngsters living together while studying who form a kind of surrogate family. Inviting more people into this definition opens us up to a wider social commensality.

HOW DOES COMMENSALITY CHANGE WHEN WE WIDEN THE SOCIAL CIRCLE AT A COMMENSAL OCCASION TO INCLUDE NON-FAMILY MEMBERS?

Morten: There are several kinds of commensality, and we've been discussing families so far. But having an outsider eat at the family table is a strong demonstration of trust and the wish to make this person feel at home. We change the setting from a family dinner table to creating a commensality of strangers wishing to form a group and demonstrate trust at a slightly different level.

Susanne: The type of commensality shown depends very much on the occasion, such as if the stranger is a friend of the kids, friend of the parents or the mother's boss: All of these would create different kinds of commensality. Some would simply be hospitable, whereas other types would be more concerned with power play or creating a "new family."

DOES COMMENSALITY NEED A TABLE TO TAKE PLACE, OR CAN IT BE MORE CASUAL? ARE FORMAL MEALS IMPORTANT?

Susanne: Sitting on the couch and watching TV while eating isn't commensality. It requires that the people concentrate on each other and the food.

> The reason we have societies is so that we can be better together than any individual member can be alone.

Morten: This is a difficult question. Eating together spontaneously can elicit the feeling of being a strong group, but a small degree of formality is probably required. Human groups are rarely informal or casual: We're a strongly hierarchical species, and so-called "informality" often involves a lot of highly formal—albeit subconscious—rules about who wishes an event to begin, who can sit where and who the "leader" or the most desirable person is. That feeling of being part of a group is almost impossible without hierarchies, even if they're sometimes completely implicit. At formal dinners, such substrata are more often expressed explicitly.

HOW CAN COMMENSALITY BE USED TO REDUCE OR ELIMINATE HIERARCHIES?
Morten: I don't think it can. What it can do is highlight the existence and importance of hierarchies. By instilling a consciousness of hierarchy, maybe this could lead to criticism and a change for the better.

WHEN EDITING *COMMENSALITY*, WHAT WERE YOU THE MOST SURPRISED TO LEARN?
Morten: I was interested by the fact that looking at food as a way of keeping healthy—as a kind of fuel for your body or medicine for your ills—is actually very bad for you, because it counteracts food's social importance as part of commensality. That was an eye-opener for me.

WHY AREN'T MORE PEOPLE TALKING AND WRITING ABOUT THE ACT OF COMMENSALITY?
Morten: It's because the academic environment involved with food has mostly been biology, chemistry and medicine. As I said before, they regard food as fuel for an individual body and disregard the fact that humans are social animals and not bodies. To some of them, food is stuff that could be replaced by pills—if good enough pills were available. Instead, our book presents research mainly from three very different areas of study: archaeology, anthropology and history of religions.

WHAT ROLE DOES FOOD AND COMMENSALITY PLAY IN DEVELOPING OUR PERSONAL IDENTITIES?
Morten: What we eat and don't eat is part of our identity. At a communal table, the food patterns of our culture are learned and place us within a group. Commensality is often an occasion for displaying a culture's hierarchy and making this explicit. For instance, children might sit at the end of the table, the eldest woman might be expected to serve, etc. This provides identity and belonging.

WHAT ROLE DOES COMMENSALITY PLAY IN TERMS OF EXPRESSING A NATIONAL IDENTITY?
Susanne: The concept of a nation is artificial, so it's always created. There's nothing natural about the notion of what makes a nation a nation, so food can help people create one. Certain dishes are either purposefully created as a national dish or are developed into one.
Morten: This is mainly through the foods eaten at a common table and the rules surrounding how they're eaten. There's a pattern to follow: a hierarchy of foods and the order in which they're eaten. This is different in different countries—even in different parts of countries. For example, a Danish luncheon is a highly

> To eat in the company of others is a strong expression of trust and "togetherness" of a much higher order than just "being together."

formalized affair. The bread is always hard rye bread. Certain dishes are indispensable: There must be pickled herring—this is eaten first on special plates. There should be cold cuts, which are eaten separately, not together. There might be a warm dish, which could be liver paste, and cheese must finish the meal. This order cannot be reversed. This is formal, but most Danes would just consider it proper. However, it distinguishes Danes and creates Danes at the same time. Another prime example is the American Thanksgiving dinner: the turkey, the stuffing, the gravy, the cranberry jelly, apple pie, pumpkin pie. It's much the same.

WHAT KIND OF DINNER TABLES DID YOU GROW UP EATING AROUND?

Susanne: My family ate supper together on weekdays and all meals together on weekends—I never enjoyed the early Sunday breakfasts! In Germany, schools finish at 1 or 2 p.m., so my mother always made hot lunch, which I warmed up when I got home from school.

Morten: We had dinner together every single night. The food was always good, always carefully prepared and often discussed and praised—by the grown-ups. There was always conversation and children were allowed to participate, but they weren't expected to. We would be allowed to leave the table early because the grown-ups just went on and on talking! There was an emphasis on finishing and not wasting, which I didn't enjoy—you were coerced to try as hard as you could to eat everything. Pig's liver is one of those things I remember vividly as a problematic food; it was my mother's favorite dish, so she served it once a month.

AS ADULTS, WHAT ARE SOME OF YOUR PERSONAL TRADITIONS WHEN IT COMES TO COMMENSALITY?

Morten: Now I just live with my partner, and we eat together at the table every night. Both of us were brought up like that, and neither of us could imagine it differently. We always did it that way as our children were growing up too: There was no excuse for not being at the table. Then again, we rarely had to make excuses, because we all wanted to be at the table with each other. The table was also a place where issues were brought up. It could be a small battleground, but not often.

Susanne: I cook every evening when I come home, and my husband and I always eat together at the table. I enjoy cooking—it's my way to separate working from being at home.

WHAT SIMPLE CHANGES CAN WE MAKE IN ORDER TO CREATE A BETTER SENSE OF COMMENSALITY AROUND OUR DINNER TABLES?

Morten: We should stress the importance of the food we eat: not how healthy it is, but how good it tastes and what labor went into making it. This means not buying take-out too often, trying foods that you don't like and expanding what you eat. It's important because it makes us more critical, and this is the road to improving quality. The idea of cooking a communal meal for and with strangers is a good way to enhance commensality.

HOW CAN WE BRING MORE COMMENSALITY INTO OUR LIVES?

Morten: By eating together more! Finally, a simple question with a simple answer!

WORDS
STEPHANIE ROSENBAUM KLASSEN

PHOTOGRAPHS
DOMINIK TARABANSKI

STYLING
ALPHA VOMERO

Making

Believe

In celebration of the make-believe stories we once believed, this photo essay is a tribute to the fibs and fables that taught us how to wonder.

Logic takes a looser form when you're still figuring out the shape of the world. Magical thinking makes sense: Why wouldn't pushing on the back of the seats help a car get up the hill? If voices come out of the radio, surely there are tiny people living inside it? And how sad was it that people in old movies had to live in a world that was only black-and-white? Life is livelier when you're five, after all: Every stuffed animal has its own personality, marbles and LEGOs form armies and alliances, and no one understands you better than your dog—except maybe your imaginary friend. While our parents and older siblings could've been straight with us, admitting that eating our crusts *wouldn't actually* make our hair curl

and our faces *wouldn't really* stay like that when the wind changed, instead they used these whimsical tales to soothe our fears and coddle our fantasies. Sometimes these made-up stories were told out of kindness or Mom-knows-best consideration, like the one about the sick pet who went on permanent holiday with his buddies at that farm upstate or the jingling ice-cream truck that was always fresh out of popsicles right before dinner. As sensible as we may become in later years, we never really want to lose our willingness to believe in make-believe. Whether it means cheering for computer-generated dinosaurs in 2015 or ogling the strange creatures in Ripley's Odditorium in the 1930s, constantly questioning what's

true and false—and then not minding which is which—is a human joy. Reality, they may have thought, would intrude soon enough. So why not let imagination and creative invention reign for a little while longer? By our elders telling us these stories or letting us make up our own, they encouraged us to be curious and let our imaginations run free, questioning everything. And now, all grown up, it's our turn to continue the narrative by telling tall tales of chocolate-milk cows, recounting the little girl who grew a watermelon in her belly and smiling together at the man in the moon: Remembering the stories we once believed and passing them down to the children we know keeps that sense of wonder alive. For all of us.

"In fairyland, they have cotton candy for clouds—that's why as soon as you put it in your mouth, it tastes sweet, then disappears."

"If you and your friends keep carrying on like that all night instead of sleeping, you're going to wake up *the thing...*"

"Don't eat too fast—if you swallow a watermelon seed, it won't be long until one starts growing in your stomach."

"Oh no, *of course* Goldie didn't die: Fish just change color as they get older."

"If normal milk comes from white cows and chocolate milk comes from brown ones, then all candy must come from rainbows."

"Eating too much chocolate before bedtime gives you nightmares, so perhaps it's best to give it to me for safekeeping."

"Your dolls come alive when you're asleep, but they're so shy that if you open your eyes, they'll freeze again."

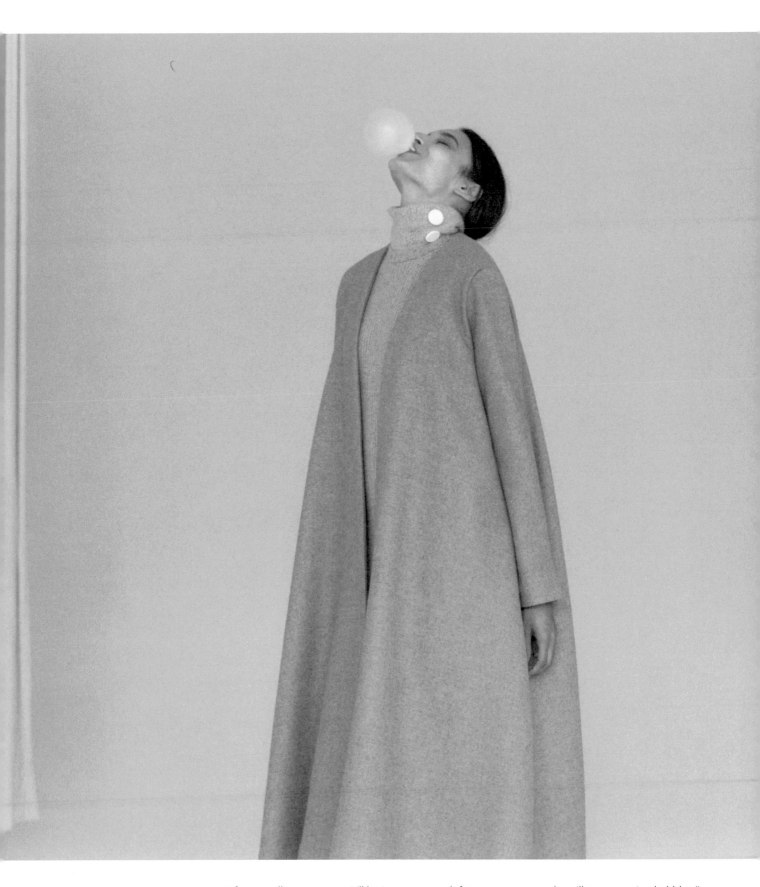

"If you swallow your gum, it'll be in your stomach for seven years... and you'll start sneezing bubbles."

RECIPES
DIANA YEN

PHOTOGRAPHS
ANDERS SCHØNNEMANN

STYLING
MIKKEL KARSTAD & SIDSEL RUDOLPH

The Blood
Menu

When we think of blood relatives, we consider comfort food, handed-down recipes and sharing meals with our families. While these recipes don't get too bloody—there's no rare steak, blood pudding or haggis—we found inspiration in thinking about our lifeblood to create this scarlet-splattered feast.

NEW YORK
GINGER SOUR

*This crimson-hued cocktail mixes some
of our favorite flavors: wine, whiskey
and ginger, with a bright splash of lemon.
Bloody good.*

2 ounces (60 milliliters) rye or
  bourbon whiskey
1 ounce (30 milliliters) Ginger Simple
  Syrup (recipe below)
¾ ounce (20 milliliters) fresh lemon juice
½ ounce (15 milliliters) dry, full-bodied
  red wine, such as Malbec or Syrah

Combine the whiskey, simple syrup and lemon juice in a cocktail shaker.
Fill with ice, cover and shake well. Strain the cocktail into a rocks glass filled
with ice. Carefully pour the wine over the back of a spoon held just above the
surface of the drink, allowing the wine to float on top. Serve immediately.

MAKES ABOUT 1 ½ CUPS (360 MILLILITERS)

GINGER
SIMPLE SYRUP

*Sugar. Water. Fresh ginger. That's all
you need to make this sweet beverage mixer.
No need to buy simple syrup when making
it at home is so, uh, simple.*

1 cup (200 grams) sugar
1 cup (240 milliliters) water
4 ounces (115 grams) fresh ginger, peeled
  and thinly sliced (about ¾ cup)

In a small saucepan, bring the sugar and water to a boil over medium-high
heat, stirring to dissolve the sugar. Add the ginger, remove the pan from the
heat and set aside to steep for 30 minutes. Strain the syrup through a sieve
and discard the ginger. Cool completely before using. The syrup can be kept
refrigerated in an airtight container for up to 1 month.

SAVORY FIG AND GOAT CHEESE TART WITH POMEGRANATE GLAZE

Fruit and cheese should never be confined to dessert. The Pomegranate Glaze adds a Middle Eastern element to this rich and decadent tart—adjust the figgyness and glaze drizzling to your liking.

FOR THE CRUST

½ cup (55 grams) toasted walnuts

1 ½ cups (195 grams) all-purpose flour, plus more for rolling

1 teaspoon salt

½ teaspoon granulated sugar

½ cup (1 stick/115 grams) cold unsalted butter, cubed, plus more for greasing

1 large egg

FOR THE POMEGRANATE GLAZE

1 cup (240 milliliters) pomegranate juice

1 tablespoon honey

½ teaspoon cornstarch

FOR THE FILLING

8 ounces (225 grams) fresh goat cheese, at room temperature

½ cup (120 milliliters) heavy cream

2 large egg yolks

1 ½ tablespoons fresh lemon juice

1 teaspoon grated lemon zest

½ teaspoon salt

¼ teaspoon black pepper, freshly ground

15 fresh figs, preferably Black Mission, quartered

FOR THE CRUST

In a food processor, pulse the walnuts until finely ground. Add the flour, salt and sugar and process to combine. Scatter the butter over the dry ingredients and pulse until the mixture resembles coarse cornmeal.

In a small bowl, whisk the egg with 1 teaspoon of cold water. While pulsing the food processor, slowly drizzle the egg mixture through the feed tube until the dough comes together. Turn the dough out onto a floured work surface and lightly knead it into a flattened disk. Wrap the dough tightly in plastic wrap and refrigerate until cold, at least 30 minutes, or up to 1 day.

Grease a 10-inch (25-centimeter) round tart pan with butter and coat it lightly with flour, tapping out the excess. Using a rolling pin, roll out the dough to a ¼-inch (6-millimeter) thickness on a lightly floured work surface. (It should be about 2 inches (5 centimeters) greater in diameter than the tart pan.) Carefully transfer the dough to the pan, and gently press it into the bottom and sides. Trim the excess dough hanging over the edges with a knife, and prick holes all over the bottom of the dough with a fork. Wrap it in plastic wrap and freeze until very cold, at least 30 minutes.

Preheat the oven to 375°F (190°C). Remove the tart pan from the freezer. Place the tart pan on a baking sheet, fit a piece of parchment paper against the surface of the dough, and weigh the parchment with baking weights or dried beans. Bake for 20 minutes. Remove the weights and parchment paper and bake until lightly browned, about 10 minutes more. Let cool slightly.

FOR THE POMEGRANATE GLAZE

In a small saucepan, bring the pomegranate juice and honey to a boil over medium-high heat. Cook until reduced by half, 5 to 7 minutes. In a small bowl, stir the cornstarch with 2 teaspoons cold water until smooth. Whisk the cornstarch mixture into the pomegranate reduction, then continue boiling the sauce until thickened and syrupy, 1 to 2 minutes. Cool completely.

FOR THE FILLING

Turn the oven temperature down to 350°F (180°C). In a food processor, combine the goat cheese, cream, egg yolks, lemon juice, lemon zest, salt and pepper until smooth. Transfer the cheese mixture to the crust and smooth the surface with a spatula, spreading it evenly.

Bake the tart until the filling is just set but before the top begins to brown, 20 to 25 minutes. Cool slightly, then arrange the figs in concentric rings to cover the tart, cut sides up. Drizzle the figs and tart with as much Pomegranate Glaze as you desire. Serve warm or at room temperature.

RED VELVET LAVA CAKES

Invented at New York's Waldorf Astoria in the 1930s, red velvet cake is adored by the masses. In this interpretation, molten chocolate turns into gooey lava as it oozes from the center of this soufflé-like cake.

FOR THE GANACHE

4 ounces (115 grams) semisweet
    chocolate chips
¼ cup (60 milliliters) heavy cream

FOR THE CAKE

4 ounces (115 grams) bittersweet
    chocolate, chopped
¼ cup (55 grams) unsalted butter, cubed,
    plus more for greasing
3 tablespoons all-purpose flour,
    plus more for dusting
¼ teaspoon salt
3 large eggs
½ cup (100 grams) granulated sugar
1 teaspoon pure vanilla extract
1 teaspoon red gel-paste food coloring
Confectioners' sugar, optional

FOR THE GANACHE

Place the semisweet chocolate in a small heat-proof bowl. In a small saucepan, warm the cream over medium-high heat until it just begins to boil. Pour the cream over the chocolate, let stand 2 to 3 minutes for the chocolate to soften, and then whisk until smooth. Cover with plastic wrap and refrigerate until set, about 1 hour. Using two teaspoons, form 6 balls of ganache, spacing them out on a parchment-lined tray. (The leftover ganache can be warmed and served with the finished cakes, or kept in an airtight container in the refrigerator for up to 2 weeks, or in the freezer for up to 3 months.) Freeze the ganache balls until solid, about 1 hour, or they can be wrapped tightly and kept in the freezer for up to 3 days before using.

FOR THE CAKE

Preheat the oven to 350°F (180°C) and adjust the oven rack to the middle position. Grease six 4-ounce (120-milliliter) ramekins or 6 cups of a standard muffin tin with butter and coat them lightly with flour, tapping out excess. Place them on a baking sheet and set aside.

In a small saucepan, stir together the bittersweet chocolate and butter over medium-low heat until just melted. Remove from the heat and whisk in the flour and salt until well combined.

In the bowl of an electric mixer fitted with the paddle attachment, or in a medium bowl using a handheld electric mixer, beat the eggs. Slowly add the sugar and continue mixing until the eggs are foamy and pale in color, 3 to 4 minutes. Stir in the vanilla and food coloring. Pour in the melted chocolate mixture and use a rubber spatula to stir until just combined. Divide the batter evenly among the prepared ramekins.

Place 1 ball of ganache into the center of each ramekin, taking care not to press it all the way to the bottom. The goal is to have it immersed in the center of the cake. Use a spoon to smooth the batter over the ganache.

Bake for 15 to 20 minutes, until the tops are just set. Set aside to cool for 2 to 3 minutes. Loosen the edges of the cakes with a butter knife, and then turn them out onto individual plates, or onto a baking sheet if using a muffin tin. Dust with confectioners' sugar and serve with more of the warmed ganache* on the side, if desired.

*To warm the leftover ganache, place it in a heat-proof bowl over a pot of gently simmering water and stir until melted.

WORDS
GEORGIA FRANCES KING
RACHEL EVA LIM
KELSEY E. THOMAS

ILLUSTRATIONS
CHIDY WAYNE

Profile Series:
The Creative Gene

Our families play a meaningful role in shaping our ideas, opinions and passions, so it's no wonder that they infiltrate so many creative endeavors. In this profile series, we interview writers, photographers, artists, directors and other imaginative types about their familial muses, which creative talents they inherited, which were nurtured and how they're passing on what they've learned to the next generation.

Alice Sage, Curator

Through her work at the V&A Museum of Childhood in London, this curator has developed a unique perspective on the way children are influenced by the environments around them.

The V&A Museum of Childhood is home to the U.K.'s largest selection of children's objects, including Victorian dollhouses, attendance medals and ancient stuffed animals, along with costumes, paintings and archives that document the social history of childhood in 17th-century Britain. The museum encourages children to interact with the exhibitions and has more than 460,000 visitors a year. Alice Sage discusses the universal allure of childhood objects, the qualities that inspire an imaginative and playful upbringing and how her definition of family has evolved during her time as a curator.

What does a typical day at the museum look like? — No two are the same! When I'm planning exhibitions, my days are very busy doing research about objects in the collection. This might involve working quietly in the library, visiting other archives or meeting experts and researchers at other museums. Then there's the collections side of things. When we acquire objects, I like to meet with the donors and hear about their lives and their family history. I find that fascinating. I think it's a curator's job to collect and save stories as well as objects.

What do you think it is about childhood objects that make adults want to see and interact with them? — Objects have the power to transport us back in our own lives. It often happens that visitors are taken by surprise when they see toys that can bring childhood memories flooding back. But as well as that personal connection, these objects can demonstrate larger social narratives. For example, seeing the difference in clothing, education and healthcare between the rich and poor children of the past reminds us that we have to address inequality in the present.

How has your own notion of family changed since you've been working at the museum? — Childhood is a universal experience but no two are the same, and that makes it an endlessly interesting subject to study. I've become more aware of how contingent family life is on circumstances. I was so fortunate to be born into a relatively well-off, stable home in Britain, where the state provided healthcare and education. This is a great privilege that meant I could spend my childhood mostly having a good time, learning about the world, exploring my interests and being safe and nourished. At the museum, I hear about many other types of childhoods. The idea of family has changed so much into a more open, fluid definition. This is a positive development that means the old nuclear family of heterosexual parents with biological children isn't the only way to create a context of love and support for youngsters anymore.

Are there any elements of childhood across the ages that have remained the same? — I look after the archive, which includes school exercise books, drawings and stories written by children. While reading these expressions of imagination, what strikes me most is how children of the 1840s, 1900s or 1960s are so similar. A sense of adventure,

The idea of family has changed into a more open, fluid definition. This is a positive development that means the old nuclear family of heterosexual parents with biological children isn't the only way to create a context of love and support for youngsters anymore.

curiosity and creativity comes through every time, regardless of the fact that the children's choice of words might be shaped by their education and upbringing. So there's that sense of a shared humanity, of the potential for all humans to make creative work.

What value do institutions such as the V&A Museum of Childhood add to how society understands and approaches family? — Childhood is such a culturally loaded concept, so it's important that we remember it's a historically contingent idea. Whatever the current controversy or moral panic, institutions such as the Museum of Childhood are able to put these things in context and ask where these ideas and fears come from. Views on childhood change over time, and by taking a long view, we can understand our own lives and culture more deeply.

Please tell us about your own family. — I'm the middle of three sisters, which means I had to share a lot when I was young! My parents worked long hours as they ran their own business, so I got very good at entertaining myself. My sisters and I spent a lot of time with our grandparents, so I developed a real interest in the past by listening to their stories. The women in my family have been great inspirations: They all have independent lives and interests and haven't conformed to conventional gender roles. My mother had little time for cleaning and housework, and that's definitely a tradition I'm continuing!

How did your family encourage your creativity? — There's a danger in families of children being pigeonholed into certain roles. I always felt my older sister was the "arty" or creative one. I felt there wasn't much space for me to explore painting or drawing, because that was her thing. What changed my mind was working with an amazing art teacher. He believed that every single student that came into his art room had something unique to offer, and he worked hard with each of us to find out what it was. I don't think that many families

can offer that kind of objective attention. The desire to please our parents and earn their love can get in the way of thinking about what we want and enjoy. If you feel that love depends on your constant success, it can be frightening to fail. When my parents divorced when I was 16, I became freer to be myself and explore the world on my own terms. I realized that if I wanted to do something with my life, it was only me that could make it happen.

Are all children born creative? — Children who are free to play and imagine show us how creative we all can be. The psychoanalyst D.W. Winnicott wrote a lot about the link between childhood play and adult creativity. "Happy are those whose feet are well planted on the earth and yet who keep the capacity for enjoying intense sensations," he wrote. Families can encourage this by giving children space, taking them seriously and through asking questions rather than telling them what to think and do. Curiosity is essential to creativity. REL

Doug DuBois, Photographer

The award-winning photographer discusses how family narratives provide a lens that colors the way we see the world.

American photographer Doug DuBois spent 25 years photographing his family for his first monograph, *All the Days and Nights*. The book, which he calls a visual memoir, offers an unflinching examination of the emotional tension that exists in many family relationships. For his second book, *My Last Day at Seventeen*, Doug visited an Irish housing estate over the course of five years to photograph youths on the cusp of adulthood. We speak with Doug about exposing his personal life to the public and how his family has helped inform his creative process.

What was life like for you growing up? — I grew up in the New Jersey suburbs. I had two sisters and a younger brother, and it was pretty ordinary. It was good—I was a naive white boy, comfortable, hadn't seen much of the world, that kind of thing. My parents came up from working-class backgrounds and were part of the generation that tried to make it better for their children, so they did everything they could for us. They did their best.

Please tell us more about *All the Days and Nights.* — That book contains 25 years' worth of work. I was in my early twenties when I took the earliest pictures, and I was

in my forties when I completed it. I had always photographed my family, largely because they were there. I was learning how to make pictures, so if I needed someone to sit for me because I needed to figure out a certain camera and was stumbling all over the place, who better than your mom? I had no interest in photographing my family in and of itself, but they were there, and they were nice.

Right before I went to grad school, I started to make portraits in earnest, and I also started to take photos of my family in earnest. Then my father had an accident on a commute back into Jersey from the city. It was very, very bad. He nearly died and it took about two years for him to recover. I moved back home the summer before going to grad school and kept photographing as a way to deal, a way to process. Photographing in earnest became very therapeutic. The photos from this time depicted a family sort of falling apart and having the fortitude to keep itself together. And that's the first half of the book: my father's recovery, my mother's consequential depression, their attempt to hold it together and my younger brother growing up.

And then I stopped for almost 10 years. It got too hard. I felt photographing wasn't helping anyone. I learned that there's a

difference between photographing your family and relating to them—I needed to be there. Making a photograph isn't the same as understanding what's going on: You can't be fully there for someone and photograph at the same time.

But then the body of work began to weigh me down. It was a little bit successful—it was shown at the Museum of Modern Art in New York—and I realized that I had to figure out this body of work. So I went back to the photographs. I photographed the second half of the book in my late thirties, early forties. By then my parents had divorced after 42 years, my sister had had a son and I had a very different relationship with my family.

What was the process of photographing each frame? — Most of the photographs are directed and posed—some are made in the moment, but the second half of the book is all performed. The works are less like a piece of journalism and more like a memoir. Memoirs aren't written in the moment—they're reflective. They deal with all the subjective elements and all the faults of memory. To evoke my perspective, I use artifice in my work in the same way a writer might obsess on a sentence for months in trying to write about his or her life. In

If you try to look at your family narrative honestly, hopefully you can shape it into something healthy and rewarding. That's your narrative—it's *yours*, no one else's.

that way, these photos are less like a diary and more like carefully crafted paragraphs where I want to figure how best to describe my mother's depression. I'm looking back and writing my story very subjectively from my point of view: These are my stories. These are my pictures. This is my take.

How did your family feel about you taking and publishing personal photos of them? Were they proud, or did it make them uncomfortable? — A little of both, always. In the early '90s, I remember my mother bringing all her lady friends into the Museum of Modern Art, and it was a big deal to her. But when I started working on the book much later, 20 years had passed and there was some trepidation. My parents' divorce was still kind of raw, and a book has a different kind of permanence than an exhibition. An exhibition is taken down, but a book hangs around—it's always going to be out there. By the time the book came out, my mother was beginning to have signs of dementia, so her relationship with it became somewhat complicated. She died last year, but when she was in assisted living, she showed it to people and said, "Here's my son's book."

My father was a little tenser than my mother, but he understands that the book is my story, even if he says things happened differently in his perspective. My sister and my brother feel the same way in that they understand it. They also understand the photographs don't define them. My sister's always very good about that. She says, "That's not me—that's my picture."

Do you think tension is an important part of the family dynamic? — What is family if it's not full of tension? It just depends on how you describe tension: Happiness is a certain kind of tension; joy is certainly a tension. So tension doesn't necessarily mean that things are bad. Tension has a certain dramatic notion, and it sparks a narrative. There's an emotional sort of resonance that I try to create in my work, and then viewers begin to develop and project their own story. The book has no text or captions,

so the tension you read is the tension you project from your own experiences.

How does your photography explore some of the less commonly talked about aspects of family life? — If you look at contemporary literature, film and television, families are largely dystopic and dysfunctional. There's only a few kinds of family sitcoms on television left where, at the end of the episode, everyone is smiling and happy again, but that was the model when I was growing up. So as a kid, I had no clue what family really was or meant. The catalyst was when my father fell from that train. Things changed radically. I grew up and saw my parents as human. And that's a very important rite of passage: When you realize your parents are as fucked-up as you are. And that's part of what the photography book is about: Your parents are stumbling through life, just like you.

What has your work as a photographer taught you about family that you wouldn't have learned otherwise? — With *All the Days and Nights*, people generally see my family through their family: Their own families are either like or not like my family. I think everyone sees the world that way. Family narratives are basically the narratives that you define yourself and see the world through, good or bad. What defines a family has changed and it's now quite diverse, rightly so. It would be hard to grow up or come of age without some notion of family: It's a cross-cultural, universal framework for stories to describe who you are. Maybe that's why I keep returning to photographing my family—because it's so important. You don't just walk away from it. Many people say, "Oh, I don't want to be like my mother" or "I don't want to be like my father" for whatever reason, but that narrative is still defining you, even in the negative. You can't escape it, but you don't have to. If you try to look at it critically and honestly, hopefully you can shape it into something healthy and rewarding. That's your narrative—it's *yours*, no one else's. And that's important. KET

The Lim Family, Publishers

In addition to DNA, this family shares two creative projects: an art collective called Holycrap and their zine, Rubbish.

When it's deadline time at the Lim family home in Singapore, the kitchen table is transformed into a factory for intricate folding, ink stamping and hand numbering. The end product: 300 copies of their biannual "famzine," *Rubbish*. Since launching their art collective, Holycrap, in 2011, Pann and Claire Lim and their kids, Renn and Aira, have held exhibitions, won international awards and have produced four issues of *Rubbish*. But for the Lims, their focus has stayed on passing down lessons and stories to their children. They share the ins and outs of working on projects as a family.

What's the idea behind Holycrap?

Pann: Holycrap is a family art collective consisting of my wife, Claire, our son, Renn, 11, our daughter, Aira, 9, and myself.

Claire: One night in 2011, Pann mentioned how he was always sharing insight into creativity and design with students and other creatives. And he was feeling really bad that he wasn't doing the same for our kids. We both love art, design, ideas, movies and music, and I suppose we know no other way to raise our kids than through these disciplines. He felt it was probably time for

us to embark on some kind of a "project" with Renn and Aira. We really wanted to raise the kids working on projects together, collecting all these simple but important day-to-day memories. We believe that if we take a look back at what we've done maybe after 10 years or even more, it will be really nostalgic and marvelous. The next morning we told the kids and they were like, "OK! So fun! Let's do this!" We relish this whole process of everyone working together, sharing ridiculous ideas, talking rubbish, feeling happy and even the feelings of frustration while trying to meet the deadlines. No words can describe how much closer we've become as a family after Holycrap was formed.

Why did you decide to create your "famzine" *Rubbish*?

Claire: This zine was created mainly for Renn and Aira. Hopefully 20 years down the road, they'll both look back at what we've done and will be able to fully comprehend what this was meant to be. And in the meantime, if there are friends and strangers who enjoy reading up on our shenanigans, and if that puts a smile on their faces, there's nothing

more I can wish for. When the day comes that Pann and I aren't around anymore, this is what we want to leave behind for our kids: our photos, our stories, all these zines with our adventures and memories.

What is the process of creating *Rubbish*? How do you decide as a family what to put into the magazine?

Pann: The process is quite an organic one. We start with the content we've all been collecting daily and see what's most interesting and close to our hearts. When we brainstorm together, it's likely to be in front of a pot of green tea and some light snacks, and we just chatter away. Claire and I will then pick out all the interesting insights the kids might have and we develop from there. It's very important that the kids are part of this brainstorming process.

Claire: From day one, we explained to the kids what doing this project together entails and how we value their opinions and ideas even though they're just kids. We always believe there's so much to learn from children. They often give suggestions or ideas that we wouldn't have thought about. And why shouldn't their opinions matter?

—

Creativity covers all aspects of our lives.
It definitely doesn't limit us to only being an
artist or a designer. Being creative is to know
how to solve issues or problems—how to take a
different route to get to your
desired destination.

They're also an integral part of the family. So when they were keen and wanted to embark on this path with us, we couldn't have been happier.

Renn: We'll always sit down together and discuss work or ideas until we come to a decision or conclusion. I started out drawing and painting first. I love doodling the most because it relaxes me, and I love to daydream a lot, sometimes too much. Then as I got older, I contributed more ideas and started to do more photography. I really enjoy taking photos. We don't use digital cameras because Dad explained to us that shooting on film is more exciting as we can't preview what we shoot.

Aira: We ask each other questions about what we like or don't like. We always write down or draw our thoughts and brainstorm together. Sometimes after an outing or event, we come home and just start writing down our feelings, because maybe these feelings can be used for ideas in our zines. I enjoy writing a lot, especially short stories and poems. I doodle on my school assessment papers and books—sometimes it gets me into trouble with my teachers, but Mom and Dad don't really mind as long as I finish my homework!

How do you inspire creativity in your kids?

Pann: Creativity is a way of life. The things we say, the songs we listen to, the artists we adore, the books we read, the movies and documentaries we watch, the food we prepare, the way we arrange our furniture and the solutions we choose are all a part of a subliminal way to inspire creativity in our kids.

Claire: Creativity truly covers all aspects of our lives. It definitely doesn't limit us to only being an artist or a designer or to the confines of the "art world." Being creative is to know how to solve issues or problems—how to take a different route to get to your desired destination. Teaching our kids to be creative is simply to give them the knowledge that all problems have a solution, to give them the means to overcome obstacles. At least, that's what we hope to instill in our kids.

Pann and Claire, what types of families did you grow up in?

Pann: I was very fortunate to grow up in a family of musicians—even the parrots in my mother's home have been trained to sing both English and Chinese songs!

Claire: And it's so funny how I come from the other extreme end of the spectrum: I grew up in a regular, super-normal church-going family, and the closest I got to singing was singing hymns in church and secretly singing along to my older brother's precious *Billboard Top 100 Hits* lyric book! We didn't buy any art or go to museums often. Although, my mom did tell me years later that she'd always harbored a love for drawing and creating stuff and had wanted to go to art school. But her family was poor, so joining the workforce was the only option. But now that she's enjoying her retirement years, she's doing stuff she loves, such as making small toys out of cardboard.

How did your upbringing influence you?

Claire: The most important and crucial aspect of my so-called "noncreative" growing up years was that they were actually pretty creative in the sense that my parents gave us quite a fair amount of space to grow and be ourselves. I was never a model student, but my parents never forced me to study more. When I came home with bad grades, they were disappointed, of course, but they never punished me for it. They reprimanded and scolded me, but they also encouraged me. So when I decided to pursue design, I told myself I better not disappoint them anymore. Creativity was the freedom and trust they gave me, even though it took me quite a long time to realize it.

Do you think that creativity is inherited, nurtured or a little of both?

Pann: I strongly believe that it's a mixture of both. If a singer is tone-deaf by nature, no amount of nurture can change that. If the singer is musically talented but has zero exposure, the chances of him succeeding will likely be lower too.

Claire: Of course, there are always situations where a person doesn't have any talent for, say, acting, but if she pursues it with vigor and hard work, eventually she may become a renowned actor. There are always exceptions in life, but you've really got to work for it.

Renn and Aira, by making *Rubbish* with your parents, what do you think you are learning about growing up?

Renn: I'm definitely becoming more disciplined. Because of the work that Aira and I have been doing with our family, I've learned to pay more attention in class and to ask more questions.

Aira: One big thing I've learned is how to be more patient, because I think I've always been quite impatient. Mommy used to say I couldn't sit still for long, but now I can! I now know what commitment is and how to work well with others, whether that's in school or at home. When we work on class projects in groups together at school, I listen to my friends, and when they argue, I try to stop them. Learning is something we do every day, even when we aren't doing our family projects with each other.

What's it like working on creative projects as a family? Do you think that it brings you closer together?

Renn: Family time and family bonding is the key to happiness, and doing this project together as a family gives me that opportunity. I've been learning about teamwork and how to respect other people's ideas and thoughts. Doing work together keeps us strong because we can learn so much more from each other. As long as our hearts are in this together, then everything is fun and awesome.

Aira: Throughout the process of doing all our projects, I've learned so much more about my family. We have to communicate our ideas and feelings, and sometimes we even have to disagree with each other. But we always encourage each other and continue to think further. From here, we can understand each other better. Dad always explains to us that learning is a lifelong process, and I'd like for us to continue learning from one another. KET

Ira Sachs, Filmmaker

This writer-director is contributing his distinct vision to help change the portrayal of families in the film world.

Ira Sachs' work explores the challenges and rewards that accompany familial exchanges: His latest film, *Love Is Strange*, is a multigenerational epic set in cramped New York City apartments, and he's currently filming *The Silent Treatment*, a movie about two boys who stop talking to their parents. In addition to his film work, he also runs two mentoring programs that nurture creativity in the next generation of gay creatives. We talk to him about the ways community extends beyond blood ties and how his perception of family changed when he started creating his own.

What was life like for you growing up? — I was born in Memphis, Tennessee, in 1965. My parents divorced when I was three, so my two older sisters and I were raised by our mom, but we also spent a few nights a week with our dad. In a way, it was a situation that mirrors my own as a parent at this point in my life, as I'm raising two children with my husband, and their mom lives next door to us, so we also co-parent.

Is there a particular aspect of family life that you're interested in capturing for your movies? — I'm interested in the conflict between being an individual but being part of a community, and that includes the community of a family: You're always trying to balance your own personal needs with those of the larger familial group. That creates real and dramatic conflicts in terms of balance for each of us. I'm also really questioning the definition of family in my films. Is it the family you're born into, or the family you choose to make as an adult? It goes beyond blood ties and into something that's really about love, and questioning the nature of love. Much of *Love Is Strange* is about how we're sort of constructed by the family that surrounds us: The film begins with a wedding between two men, which is kind of the endpoint of a long struggle. They share that celebration with friends and family, but that community doesn't exactly embrace them in such a full way. Our sense of self is heavily impacted by how others treat us, and as a gay man, I used to be more interested in being an individual because I didn't find a space for myself within the larger family unit. But that has shifted over time, because as the culture has shifted, so has my sense of self within a family.

The two leads in *Love Is Strange* are older gentlemen. What can we learn from older generations? — The film is mostly about the ways that one generation influences another. I hope the film encourages people to be aware of the temporality of our lives. That's a useful thing within our families—to realize that whatever conflict is at hand, at some point it will be over and that there will be another generation taking that space. And having that kind of perspective maybe allows for greater empathy for each other.

The film also deals with life transitions. What was it like transitioning from living on your own to introducing a whole family into your life in a short period of time? — I went from living alone in my apartment to living with my husband, our two kids and their mom over a weeklong period. Every Sunday night the parents [myself, my husband and the kids' mom, who now lives next door] meet to talk about the week and our relationships in order to try and understand the things that might go unspoken. Because we're not a nuclear family, we need to have really conscious moments for conversation. I find that's a good thing—it's created a good kind of philosophy of how to be parents, as we try to talk about things as they come up. When I was growing up, especially as I became an adult and got involved in romantic relationships, I was never successful at speaking the truth about what was going on. And now I'm at an age where that's very important to me: to speak about the things that are difficult and to speak about the things that are joyous. KET

Rachel LaCour Niesen, Photojournalist

The founder of Save Family Photos discusses her efforts to preserve other families' memories.

Save Family Photos, a virtual campfire where people can gather and share their stories online, has allowed Rachel LaCour Niesen to merge her interests in both personal and world histories by curating a selection of intimate family images from around the globe. Earlier this year, she took over *The New Yorker* photo department's Instagram account for Mother's Day, where she uploaded a series of photographs of family matriarchs with accompanying stories. She speaks about how her own family inspired her project.

What was your motivation for starting Save Family Photos? — I'm lucky to have two 91-year-old Southern grandmothers who love telling stories. These two women have both breathed life into my project. My Mississippi grandmother has a large, wood-paneled wall of family photos. As a child, I used to walk along that wall and stare at my family's faces. I saw my grandparents as children, my father graduating from high school, my uncle as a student in New York City, my aunt at a swim meet. I saw faces full of hopes and dreams—long before I ever existed. In those moments, I realized something powerful: My story started before me. When my grandfather died a year ago, I wanted to celebrate his life. I started scanning old photos of him,

then I posted a photo and story about him on Instagram and invited family and friends to do the same. Now I've received more than 10,000 family photos and stories from around the world!

Why is remembering to remember so important? — Remembering means much more than just jogging your own memory: Really remembering requires recounting memories over and over and over again. The tradition of oral history, of sitting around a campfire and sharing stories, is often overlooked in the digital era. It's slower. But it's what makes memories last for generations, not just for a social-media minute. When we take time to talk about our photos, we give them deeper meaning and context that can be passed along in the form of stories. Family stories make our futures richer by making our roots deeper.

What can families do to maintain their archives? — It's easy to feel overwhelmed when you think about the total number of family photos gathering dust in your own attic or basement. Just choose one photo and ask a family member what they remember. One is enough. Soon you'll discover that one leads to 10 and more family members will want to get involved. Then it's no longer a chore—it's a collaboration. There's

no convenient time to preserve your family history—just start somewhere.

Please tell us about your own family. — As a Southerner, I grew up surrounded by stories and oral history. We love to talk. In fact, we talk so much that my Midwestern husband was totally overwhelmed the first time he had holiday supper with us! We can't get enough of a good story, whether it's ours or someone else's. That's probably why I love curating other people's family stories—I'm always drawn in as if it were my own family.

How did your family encourage you to be creative? — I was a curious, creative, unconventional kid. Whenever I felt like I didn't fit in, my Mom would gently say, "Normal is a cycle on the washing machine." It reassured me that—no matter how quirky I was or how unusual I felt—"normalcy" was relative, maybe even irrelevant.

How can creativity be found in noncreative fields? — I think we're all born with creative energy. The real challenge is finding your medium and embracing it. Once you do, you'll never look back. I love this quote from Jackson Pollock: "When I say 'artist,' I mean the one who is building things—some with a brush, some with a shovel, some choose a pen." REL

Reiner Knizia, Game Designer

This game designer discusses how playing a round of Monopoly can help us better understand our families.

After spending more than two decades as an academic and helping manage a large financial company, Reiner Knizia embarked on his life's third chapter in game design, which was always closest to his heart. He has since designed numerous best-selling board and electronic games and was also recently inducted into the Gaming Hall of Fame. We chat with him about the creative thinking that underlies game design and how board games can foster better familial relations at any age.

What makes a good board game? — I like face-to-face games, so a good game is a platform that brings people together. Designing games is certainly more rewarding than developing laundry soap!

How is your job similar or different to other types of designers? — As a designer, my ambition is to create something new and innovative, not just to copy or reinvent the 20th Clue game. There's a certain discrepancy though, because while people are always on the lookout for something new, they're not really looking for something radically new—it also needs to be familiar. So a lot of what I do consists of balancing the desire to do something new with staying on the path. People have lots of opinions and you can't win them all, but

that's what art is: Art is something that you can't have an absolute opinion about. Art is always relative.

Where do you look for inspiration when designing games? — Ernest Hemingway once put it very nicely: "In order to write about life, first you must live it." And this is the most important point—to keep my eyes open and to see what is going on in the world. Because the world changes, and games are a mirror of our time.

How can playing board games together help families bond? — Playing games is a unique pastime that brings people together around one thing and one experience. Sports comes pretty close, but it's not something that can be engaged in equally by people of different ages: A 6-year-old boy and his 90-year-old grandma can't play rugby together, but games can be played on an equal level. And that is unique.

Playing board games is sometimes seen as something that children do rather than adults. What can we learn from them as adults? — I don't think that playing board games necessitates reverting to a more childish frame of mind. Adults can have a nice meal, a glass of wine and take out these games. Playing games isn't just for

children—it's something that accompanies us throughout our lives, and it's a pity that some people lose their connection to board games over the years.

When you were younger, how did your family encourage your creativity? — As a kid, it wasn't my ambition to become a professional game designer. It was just a hobby, and every child plays with board games. When you're a kid, you almost take everything that's happening in your life and make a game out of it: The game is in your mind, and you play it. However, my parents definitely encouraged my scientific background and my mathematical abilities—perhaps more than my creativity. They were happy that I managed to be successful in this career. We play games together and my mother actually keeps track of my game archives—a collection of around 2000 games. She's now very much involved in what I do, so we've managed to join forces!

Do you believe that creativity is inherited, nurtured or a combination of both? — I think it's both. At the end of the day, if you think you can, you can, and if you think you can't, you can't. You're given some abilities and you're stronger in some fields, but I believe that you have to find your own way. Creativity is relative. REL

The Sethi Siblings, Chef, Sommelier and Business Director

Karam, Sunaina and Jyotin Sethi are behind some of London's most beloved Indian restaurants. They explain how their childhood dinner parties turned them into social, food-loving adults.

Hailing from Finchley in North London, the Sethi siblings were raised in a family where lively dinner parties and stuffing their faces were part of the social fabric. Inspired by the dishes they learned to make from their mother, Meena, along with other relatives back in India, the three of them—chef Karam, sommelier Sunaina and business director Jyotin—have joined forces in adulthood to run a series of internationally acclaimed restaurants. These include Trishna, which received a Michelin Star in 2012, and Gymkhana, which won National Restaurant of the Year 2014 in the U.K., and a host of other well-known establishments in England and beyond. We met up with the siblings in London to chat about the power of cooperation and keeping it in the culinary family.

Were you guys always close as siblings?

Sunaina: Growing up, our lives always revolved around doing things as a family and eating as a family. Even though we spend so much time together already, we still try and do as much together as we can. Sundays are family afternoons: Everyone comes home to spend time with each other, and the boys will watch soccer. It's nice!

How do you separate work and play?

Jyotin: Only one of the restaurants is actually still open on Sundays, but you can't get away from work. For us, there's no separation between work and home life.

Sunaina: I still remember the first meeting where we sat down and Jyotin stopped, shook his head, smiled and said, "I can't believe the three of us are actually working together." That's the core of our lives. Sometimes we get told to stop talking about work, but when it's such a part of you, you can't help talking about it sometimes. All of the conversations still always revolve around food.

Who tells you to stop talking about work?

Karam: Mother…

Sunaina: Yeah, Mother! Because then we usually get into debates and she'll comment that we should switch off for a bit.

Karam: She came by one of the restaurants last week: She said it was very good, but maybe a bit spicy.

How has your mom's cooking influenced your restaurants?

Karam: We grew up eating her food, as well as her parents': We spent our summer holiday at our grandparents' in Delhi, and I'd always spend time hanging out in the kitchen there. They were the main influencers for the style of food in the restaurants. Mom's food was known to be the best Indian food in North London. Her dinner parties were always the best too: They had the best spread, and it was never overly spiced or spicy—just on point.

Jyotin: Our friends always loved coming over, not only because the food was really good, but because there was so much of it.

Karam: Then when we were at college, she'd send up food for us and our friends. She'd often help organize fund-raising events at our school by calling up other Indian mums to get each of them to cook a dish for big events.

Jyotin: But our dad would still say that he taught her how to cook!

Sunaina: When they were married, he'd say that she didn't know how to boil an egg.

How did those big dinner parties affect your business dynamic?

Sunaina: It's interesting to look back on how we acted growing up around those huge dinner parties: Karam was the one in the kitchen, Jyotin was the eldest so he was

mingling, and I was running around serving food and learning about people's drinks. So I think we naturally fell into our roles.

Jyotin: I didn't inherit any of the creative side, but my dad is an accountant, so I've always loved numbers and finance from a young age. That's something I always talked about with him, and it's what I've always wanted to do. And now I get to bring that back to this environment.

Do you feel yourselves taking on clearly defined roles as siblings?

Jyotin: I definitely feel like the older brother on occasions, particularly when things get heated, which naturally they do when you're running a business! There's always something stressful happening. Not just with these guys, but with other people—chefs and all their proclivities.

Sunaina: Jyotin has always been the mediator. I can also imagine that it took some time for my brothers to get over the fact that I'm their younger sister, to see through that and take me seriously.

How does being siblings influence your working relationship?

Sunaina: When you're related, you fight because you ultimately have the same end goal. Rather than tiptoeing around, you can get straight to the point and make your opinion known more quickly.

Karam: When fights happen with nonfamily, those people are more likely to leave.

Restaurant staffs are often described as being like families. How do you create community within your restaurant staff?

Karam: We tend to have lunch together before service, and then have a drink after service. We also have a quarterly meet-up.

Sunaina: The next one's going to be a good one—there's going to be a Trishna versus Gymkhana cricket match! The community is definitely important, because when you work at a restaurant, you often spend more time with those people than you do with your own families. That is especially true with our family.

How do you stay connected to your family in India?

Sunaina: We've spent a lot of time there, and we all got married there too. Spending time around our grandparents was part of our upbringing. After you turn about 13, you can be a little bit more independent and start enjoying it. Before that, you're sort of just dragged around by your parents to see your hundreds of relatives.

Jyotin: But now we're more selective: You can make your own decisions instead of being forced to sit in a room with 80 aunties. When we walk into my grandparents' house, it still feels like going home.

What did the dinner table look like when you were kids?

Karam: Eating! Stuffing our faces.

Sunaina: Loads of eating. When we were kids, there were arguments here and there, but it was always focused on the food.

In addition to a love of food, what else have you inherited from your family?

Sunaina: Aside from potbellies? Our parents are very, very social, so we definitely got the dinner party thing from them. They were constantly entertaining, and we love that. They're very generous, open, large-hearted people.

Jyotin: But we're better singers than our dad anyway. GFK

Hoppers, the Sethis' next restaurant, will open in London in October 2015.

Nathan Beard,
Artist

Born in Perth, Australia, this artist uses his family's Thai heritage to explore broader ideas about culture and identity.

Nathan Beard is part of an increasingly large generation of third-culture kids, a term that applies to the children of immigrant parents who raised their offspring in a country much different from their own. Much of his artistic practice explores his relationship with his relatives in Thailand through trying to reconcile the differences between his spiritual homeland and his birthplace in Western Australia. By using his mother and relatives as muses and touching on themes such as memory, inheritance and homecoming, he hopes viewers will more closely consider where they've come from and how their past has influenced them.

How did your parents' attitudes toward work and creativity influence you? — I'm somewhat of an outlier in my family as I'm the only one to have pursued a career in the arts. Growing up, we were very much working-class—my father was a security guard and my mother was primarily a housewife. She was able to incorporate strong elements of her Thai culture into a suburban-Australian context though, which has definitely been a massive influence on the development of my practice. For example, she's a keen gardener and has been able to successfully grow many traditional herbs

and vegetables used in Thai recipes. When I first showed pictures of her garden to my Thai friends, they thought they were looking at a patch of land in Thailand. Inside our family home, there are several domestic shrines decorated with statues of monks and the Thai royal family, and this eclectic aesthetic has definitely had a strong influence on my work as well. So in her own humble way, she was able to express herself creatively, even if it was coming from a pragmatic perspective.

How did your family encourage your creativity? — Growing up, I was always quite inquisitive, poring over books and magazines if I became obsessed with a topic, like dinosaurs. My dad had bought a set of World Book Encyclopedias that were my absolute favorite things in the world to get lost in. I liked learning, stoking my interest in new subjects, and in school I was drawn to choose electives in the arts. Sure, my mother expressed a bit of concern, especially that I was choosing to study art at a tertiary level as opposed to a subject like medicine or engineering that had clearer career objectives attached. But because I was the first person in my family to even go to college, my parents were generally

supportive, even if they may have had reservations about the path I was choosing.

Do you think that creativity is inherited, nurtured or a little of both? — I think it's pretty inseparable from a sense of curiosity about the world and a willingness to absorb yourself fully into the minutiae of what you find interesting. Being able to channel and edit this information into a sort of outcome is the part that takes time to develop.

How is the Thai notion of family different to the predominant beliefs in Australia? How did your parents reconcile these different values while bringing you up? — My concept of family never felt vastly different from that of my friends and classmates while growing up, but there's a concept called *bun khun* that's particular to Thai culture. It refers to an indebtedness toward those who have cared for you; a favor repaid without hesitation. This concept generally refers to the relationship between parents and children, but can be applied to other cross-generational relationships involving teachers and employers, for example. Incorporating my mother into my work as a subject and collaborator seems an organic extension of this concept of bun khun.

There's a concept called *bun khun* particular to Thai culture. It refers to an indebtedness toward those who have cared for you; a favor repaid without hesitation.

As someone who was raised in a culture different from their parents' home country, what has your experience as a third-culture kid been with finding the middle ground between your parents' expectations, your family in Thailand's expectations and your own wants and whims when it comes to determining your sense of individuality? — The idea of community established in Perth among Thai expats seems very strong—they've been able to provide a strong context to preserve traditional culture in a foreign context. Through going to temple, I could see there was a unique quality to my childhood by observing and taking part in the rituals and customs associated with Buddhism. I feel a deep sense of connection to and respect for my mother's Thai heritage, and it's definitely an invaluable part of how I identify culturally.

Your 2013 solo exhibition, "Obitus," was based entirely on your mother's relationship to her brother and her hometown. How did this project change your own relationship with your mother? — "Obitus" was the result of a residency in Bangkok. During the time of my residency, my mother's brother was diagnosed with terminal cancer. He lived next door to the house in her home province of Nakhon Nayok, which my mother abandoned after her mother died in 1992. My mother, who hadn't visited this boarded-up house for nearly 10 years, went back to spend time with him. I created a body of work about the act of her revisiting her former home, using her as the subject in the form of video and photography. It required a massive amount of bravery and openness on my mother's behalf to allow herself to be depicted so candidly. Making art in this context allowed me to form a deeper bond of trust between us and gain a deeply rewarding insight into her history and relationships that I might not have asked about otherwise. My subsequent exhibition "Ad Matres" in 2015 took further inspiration from the dusty and broken portraits of family members I discovered when searching through my mother's old house. I created a series of works named after these deceased relatives where these portraits were embellished with delicate patterns of crystals. By hand-embellishing them, I intimately acquainted myself with them while subtly referencing the kitsch-inspired aesthetic that my mother used in her domestic Buddhist shrines.

Which of your other art projects have had a particularly strong connection to the notion of family identity? — My work "Avunculus, Vale" was inspired by rigorous documentation I had taken of my uncle's funeral during the research for "Obitus." With this work, I was granted intimate access to Thai funeral customs and rituals, and I wanted to produce something that reflected upon the fundamental differences in approach to death between Thai and Western cultures for a group exhibition called "Memento Mori" in 2014. In line with Buddhist beliefs, death isn't seen as an end point, but merely a part of the cycle of life and rebirth. The work tries to process the intimacy of these traditions and acts as a memorial to my uncle.

How do your close relatives feel about being personally represented in your artwork? — As the concerns of my research have shifted to focus primarily on ideas of memory, cultural legacy and identity, my family's history has been hugely influential as a wellspring of material to draw upon. There's a complete openness on their behalf, especially among my Thai relatives, in letting me use their stories and images within my work. Allowing audiences and strangers into this personal space indicates a massive trust.

What have you learned about the concept of family through delving into the subject so heavily for your art? — Family has been a great tool to dig into the past in order to clarify broader themes that I believe have universal applications. In unpacking the structure and intimacy of family relationships, this helps to create an empathetic understanding of how culture, history and intimacy are shared between people. GFK

Binke Lenhardt, Architect

The cofounder of Crossboundaries, an architecture firm based in Frankfurt and Beijing, explains how spaces can foster creativity in children.

At Family Box in Beijing, children can hop between swimming, playing music, whooshing down a wavy slide or "shopping" for produce in a pint-size store. The initial idea behind Family Box, an early childhood education center that opened in 2013 with six branches across China, came from a Chinese businesswoman with two kids of her own. We speak to architect Binke Lenhardt about how she helped bring these creative spaces that appease children and adults alike into fruition.

Why is it important to create spaces where children and adults are treated equally? — In Europe, children are trained to be independent very early, but kids in China are more protected and mostly accompanied by a grown-up, even when they're older. Another factor that plays into this is China's one-child policy: A single child receives a great amount of attention from his or her whole family, so not only does a mother or a father often follow the child around, but the grandparents do too. This made learning spaces fill up with grown-ups rather than children. The conclusion was to design spaces where adults and children can be together, but both their needs are addressed equally. Initially grown-ups entered the space with curiosity, maybe doubt, but children took it over naturally, explored it and made it their own. I have a child who's now seven years old who experienced

Family Box when he was very small and spends time there enjoying himself.

How does Family Box find a balance between designing with kids and adults in mind? — We designed a lounge area where grown-ups can sit and have coffee while children climb within the play frame—a visual connection to the play frame is maintained so parents are encouraged to let their children play while still being in close vicinity. We also cut seating areas out of the walls so parents can sit and take a bit of distance from their playing child while still being able to see them.

What are some of the mistakes made when designing schools? — Although some new educational approaches are adjusting learning environments, most of our schools provide few innovative spaces. The conventional classroom setup is a spatial translation of an educational system that's woefully outmoded, and it often proves to be static, monofunctional and teacher-oriented. A creative learning space should be student-oriented and offer the flexibility to adapt to different scenarios.

Is creativity inherited, or can it be learned and encouraged by schools and learning environments? — Children are naturally creative, but they often outgrow their creative abilities over the years because our

educational systems simply don't value creative subjects as highly as other academic skills. Nevertheless, there's a growing consensus that creativity should be embraced and cultivated as a part of a child's development. In order to do this, we need a fundamental reform of our educational systems in terms of curriculum, teaching methods and learning environments, and the latter is where we try to contribute as architects.

Why is it so important to encourage creativity in children? — Creativity is a form of self-expression: It enables children to approach tasks from different perspectives, think outside of the box and make their own choices. This nurtures their cognitive, emotional, social and physical development, and benefits their growth as whole beings. After all, the children of today are the grown-ups of tomorrow, and in order to enable them to cope with the complexities and challenges of the modern world, it's more important than ever to teach them to think creatively and come up with innovative approaches to problem solving. As architects, we strongly believe that a built environment can either suppress or ignite creativity. By providing an age-appropriate, secure, inclusive, interactive, curiosity-raising and multisensory environment, we're not only encouraging the development of physical, cognitive, emotional and social skills, we're encouraging creativity. KET

Benjamin Law, Writer

After using his own family as fodder for his books—and now a TV show—this writer talks about how his relationship with his kin has evolved over the years.

Writing about friends and family is one of the most dangerous territories a writer can enter. However, Sydney-based writer Benjamin Law has managed to make a career out of it (without being disowned). After starting out by penning stories for magazines at age 17, he wrote his first memoir, *The Family Law*, in 2010, and *Gaysia: Adventures in the Queer East* in 2012, both of which poke fun at himself and the oddity of the world around us. With *The Family Law* recently optioned for a TV series in Australia, we spoke with the award-winning author about his kooky family, his creative upbringing and what it's like to take your dirty laundry public.

While writing *The Family Law*, how did you begin to see your family in a different light? How did you decide where to draw the line with what to divulge and what to keep private? — One of the most rewarding things about writing *The Family Law* was discovering all this stuff I didn't know about my family. Everyone assumes memoir is the easiest form of writing as

you know the story already, but you soon discover there are massive holes in your knowledge. As for what to include and what to exclude, I only had one rule: the stories had to be moving or funny. Everything else got cut. Also, David Sedaris has a good rule: If you depict someone as a buffoon, make sure you paint yourself as a bigger one. Otherwise you just look like a jerk.

The Family Law is becoming a TV show in Australia. How did it feel to invite a team of non–blood relatives into your personal narrative? — Tony Ayres—who's filmmaking royalty in Australia—is someone whose career I admired as a youngster long before we became mates. So when he said he wanted to buy the rights to *The Family Law*, I was his. As executive producer of the show, he helped assemble the best team of people, including my producer and show runner Sophie Miller. Everyone who worked on the show together had the same wrong sense of humor—I think that if you laugh at the same stuff, you're probably going to work well together.

To get meta for a moment: What kind of relationship has formed between your real family and the actors who play your TV family? — This is my first time writing for TV, so it was weird enough seeing words and scenes I'd written get translated to the screen. Then there's another level of weirdness, seeing actors play characters with the names of your family members. So it's a lasagna of weirdness—a turducken of weirdness even. I was so nervous about my family coming on to the set. I was discombobulated enough about the idea of having actors play my family members, and I had no idea how my family would react. It's insane right? "Hey, Mum, Dad and sibs! So I've written a TV show, and here are some strangers who are going to act out our lives on national television! *Good times.*" But when my family visited the set, it was possibly one of the most joyous experiences of my life. The actors were so thrilled to meet the real-life people who inspired their characters. And because the characters are at least a decade younger than all of us, the real Laws felt weirdly protective of our actor

It's hard to control five kids, so my parents were just stoked if we came home happy and had our limbs intact. Their general attitude was: Do what you love, as long as you're good at it and can make a living from it. It's good advice.

counterparts. The fact that the actors are so attractive also helped put our minds at rest, not that anyone will admit it.

Is it possible for people who think they didn't inherit the creative gene to succeed just by persevering? — It depends on your definition of success. For some people, writing one really decent song—just one— is what they aspire to. For me, it's about making a living from writing. And in order to make a living from it, you have to work damn hard. Be prepared to give up weekends. Forget public holidays. The rest is about talent, practice, instinct and—this is a controversial thing to say—good taste. And you can only develop your taste by reading, watching and experiencing a lot of art. You want to make good radio? Listen to a lot of radio. Want to be a dancer? See a lot of dance. Good writing relies on good reading too.

How did your family encourage your creativity as a kid? — I come from a pretty nontypical Chinese family. One way they showed this was by encouraging creativity. Books were never a waste of money in our home. And while my cousins were basically forced to become accountants and engineers, we were the free-range, organic kids of the local Chinese community. I guess it's hard to control five kids, so my parents were just stoked if we came home happy and had our limbs intact. Their general attitude was: Do what you love, as long as you're good at it and can make a living from it. It's good advice. None of their kids are engineers, doctors or lawyers—though, as my mother points out, a doctor would have been handy at her age, and a lawyer would have been handy during her divorce!

How does the Chinese notion of family differ from the typical Australian one? — My parents always oscillated between thinking Australian culture was awesome— democracy; multiculturalism!—and thinking it was horrendous, like the time I got my eyebrow pierced at 18. One big difference between the two cultures is respecting your elders. It's very Australian to challenge authority, which is great when it comes to pouring scorn on politicians. But when my parents saw Australians disrespect parents or the elderly, they were having none of it.

When do you feel that the idea of "family" resets and you begin making your own? — I've been with my boyfriend [Australian folk-pop musician Scott Spark] for more than a decade now—that's like centuries in gay years—and it hasn't felt as much like making a new family as expanding my existing one. In contrast to my sprawling family, after Scott's dad passed away, it was just him and his mum. So we have Christmas together, our families look out for both of us and he gives my little sisters life advice.

Your boyfriend must use a lot of his personal experiences in his songwriting. After putting your family so publicly in the spotlight, how do you feel knowing you're the subject of some of Scott's songs? — It's shallow, but I'll honestly forgive Scott anything as long as he doesn't shave off his facial hair. GFK

WORDS
ADRIENNE MATEI

PHOTOGRAPHS
MAIA FLORE

Neighborhood: Playgrounds

A playground is a cross-generational neighborhood essential where toddlers learn about balance, teenagers awkwardly coexist, old folks play chess and frazzled parents decompress. We consider the role these structures play in both our childhood development and social interactions.

Much like a swirly cone of soft-serve or a book by Roald Dahl, a good playground's whimsy delights at any age. As the destination of the weekday post-dinner amble and the Saturday settle-in alike, playgrounds acknowledge the value of the small daily pleasures that make neighborhoods feel like home. Although playgrounds have nooks, quirks and specific daisy constellations that make them unique, their basic components are near universal: the sound of collective giggles, the metallic smell that swing-set chains leave on hot palms and the sight of neighbors and neighborhood kids all festively gathered in the fresh air. At their best, playgrounds are the community sweet spot—an anytime locale with as many functions as imagination affords.

In postwar Europe, an abundance of public playgrounds sprung up in previously bombed-out lots, which the Dutch architect Aldo van Eyck described as a "true extensions of the doorstep": He transformed many of these formerly derelict spaces into lively hubs of societal healing where neighbors could socialize as their kids scrambled up climbing structures to survey their reclaimed communities.

Meanwhile, across the ocean, New York City Parks Commissioner Robert Moses was installing 658 concrete arenas that somewhat grimly epitomized the playground's American form to this day: a swing set, a ladder of monkey bars and the stark backslash of a seesaw spaced so far away that it may as well be in quarantine. Without postwar recovery to consider, utility and vandal resistance were Moses' goals, as was the installation of hundreds of those bossy public signs that preface a litany of fun-sounding ideas ("Clambering into the fountain!" "Roughhousing!") with a bold, caps-locked "NO."

Moses' tenure gave way to a freer approach when Thomas P. Hoving, the 34-year-old former Metropolitan Museum curator, replaced him in 1966. Upon his appointment, Hoving declared, "The old rinky-dink, hand-me-down stereotype of the park is out, *out!*" His new plan for parks attempted to mimic the European practice of "participatory play," where kids find stimulation from unpredictable landscapes and movable parts. To help him realize his vision, he invited architect Richard Dattner to design North America's first rebellious Adventure Playground, which was made up of previously verboten tunnels, pyramids, zip lines and things that squirt water. "A park is like a stage," Hoving proclaimed, ushering in an era of spontaneous public community events in Central Park, ranging from picnics and parties to midnight meteor viewings. "If you leave it sitting, nothing good is going to happen," he said.

Half a century later, Canadian playground architect Jeff Cutler dropped by the Garden City Play Environment he designed to find seniors in the skate park doing tai chi. It was a pleasant surprise

These photographs were taken at the Helen Diller Playground in San Francisco, California. It was designed by Koch Landscape Architecture, a firm located in Portland, Oregon, and was installed in Mission Dolores Park in 2009. Its pastel landscape features a 45-foot (14-meter) wavy slide, a sand garden, a special area for two to five year olds, climbing stones, a swing set that looks out across the playground's expanse and other treats for young and old alike.

for Cutler, who defines a playground's success by the diversity of those who enjoy it. To ensure wide appeal, playground design firms such as Cutler's Space2place and Portland, Oregon's Koch Landscape Architecture have begun to collect community input—including children's—regarding what constitutes fun. For Koch, this process resulted in the installation of a fast and wavy 45-foot (14-meter) metal slide in its 2009 redesign of San Francisco's Helen Diller Playground. The slide is accessed either by a path or by climbing up a rocky slope and is beloved by parents just as eager to fling up their arms and yell *whee!* as their kids.

Additionally, ageless design elements such as benches, strategic pathways and picnic tables provide everyone with a sense of belonging. Aligned with van Eyck's "extended doorstep" concept, the playground's role as the universal setting for a nice day is best fulfilled when it generously and simultaneously satisfies the needs of many: lounging teens, game adults, exultant children and older folks basking on sunny benches as new generations remind them of the past. Then, of course, there's the playground's most vital task: providing irresistible channels of delight for children, whose laughter imbues a playground with its soul.

Kids need to play; it's an intrinsic human behavior with the seemingly paradoxical trait of being at once blissfully aimless and critical for development. Children learn to cooperate, foster relationships and regulate emotion through playing. They develop motor skills, hone their judgment and get healthy exercise. A Canadian study from 2007 on the role of play in constructing the social brain found it strengthens the prefrontal cortex, which promotes self-reflection, creativity and empathy. Plus, kids are reportedly happiest when they're playing. In hopes of improving childhood downtime and maximizing happiness, modern scholars have taken an interest in how and why kids develop into secure and well-adjusted adults through play. One significant recent finding is that children enjoy the most physical and mental benefits from playgrounds that aren't as safe as possible, but actually only as safe as necessary.

In her 2011 thesis, "Risky Play from an Evolutionary Perspective: The Anti-Phobic Effects of Thrilling Experiences," Norwe-

gian professor Ellen Sandseter believes hyper-harmless play spaces and an exaggerated focus on safety encourages "delicate blossom disorder" in today's chronically overprotected kids. She says that when children are given the opportunity to experience exhilarating, stimulating play and the relatively benign dangers of heights, scrapes and sand-to-eye flinging, they may avoid phobias later in life.

Dr. Mariana Brussoni, an injury prevention expert at the University of British Columbia, also insists on the adaptive value of risk: "Because standardized playgrounds are so uniform, children don't need to think as much and challenge themselves to play," she says. "For example, climbing a ladder with equally spaced rungs is very different from climbing a tree where you have to think about whether you can reach the next branch, whether it'll hold your weight and whether you can jump or get back down." Risk and intrigue—whether found in vertiginous climbing structures, fast slides or movable elements—foster creativity and a sense of adventure. A good playground inoculates against fear with a preventative dose: The kids who climb the highest have progressively developed the assuredness to do so, and the kids who pop their bubble wrap realize they're not so fragile after all.

Brussoni's use of the tree as an example of playground equipment dovetails with another increasingly important element of modern playground design: nature.

The desire to run wild like mini Tom Sawyers is very good both for children's health and for that of the planet. Lack of access to natural play spaces results in "biosphere estrangement"—something a 2014 Stockholm study thoroughly examined in its analysis of 134 uniformly funded preschools. The study showed that the more time we spend as kids sinking our feet into soft moss, obscuring ourselves in lilac thatches, ripping up root beds and accidentally killing tadpoles by trying to "save them" from nothing and then crying over their tiny alien-sperm corpses, the more likely it is that we'll form a spiritual, emotional and cognitive connection with the natural world around us.

It's every generation's responsibility to foster a love of nature in its children. This can be easily accomplished by invoking three magic words: "Go play outside."

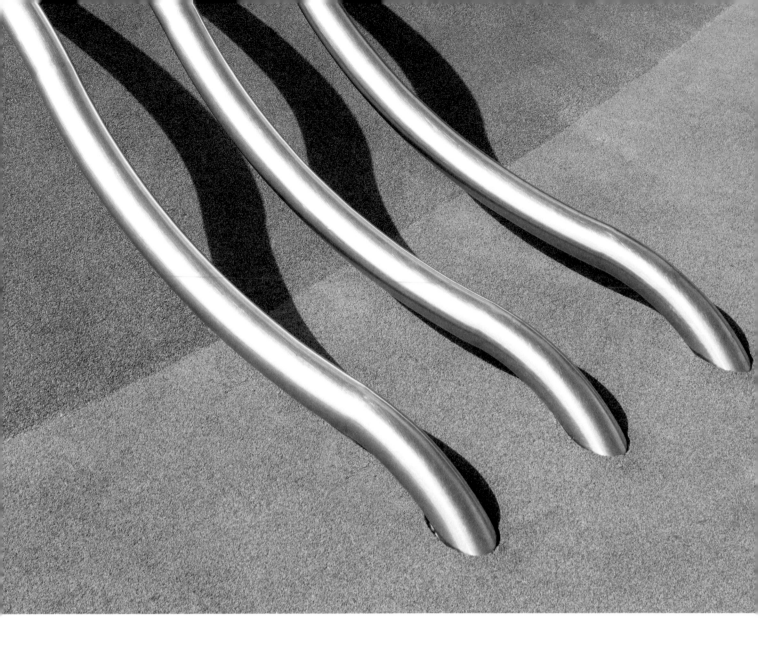

Adam Bienenstock runs a design company that uses natural materials to build custom playgrounds that reflect his clients' nearest wilderness, be it with climbable boulders of locally occurring granite or region-specific foliage. By making these structures, he strives to make nature accessible to all. "If modern kids are typically spending one hour outside and seven hours a day looking at screens, we'd better make sure that one hour connects them to something important," he says.

Given their shared enthusiasm for encouraging children to get outside, Canadian environmental luminary Dr. David Suzuki collaborates with Bienenstock through his foundation. In his most recent memoir, Letters to My Grandchildren, 79-year-old Suzuki urges his youngest family members to seize their youth by playing in puddles and parks, just as he once did. He hopes this will inspire a lifelong passion in them to safeguard a world where there will always be ladybugs to cup in hands and leafy branches to transform into the scepters of make-believe wizards. But as Suzuki explains, there's even more than environmentalism at play. "Aside from the exposure to the outside—which I feel is really critical—what playgrounds do is provide a gathering place," he says. "I have a seven-month-old grandson, and it's wonderful when I babysit because we go to the neighborhood park, I push him on a swing and I chitchat with the other children's parents. There's a real sense of community.

That's what we need: chances to get to know the people around us."

Playgrounds can transform cold, calculated city life into a warm environment where all are welcome. These spaces encourage and delight, designed as if a blueprint-wielding architect surveying their grounds had murmured, "The arch of this jungle gym must evoke a rocket ship, this tiny nook is the perfect size for a mud-pie bakery, elders will keep a watchful eye on the sandbox from here and these blackberry patches will produce just enough fruit to stain a sweet-tooth violet." A playground is a riotous oasis reflecting our sweetest, simplest value: that whether it's in a skate park or soft grass, with a tall slide or a tree stump, we all need to have a little fun.

Kinfolk
Gatherings

Our Kinfolk event series in 2015 has revolved around the idea of slowing down our sped-up lives. "Slowing down isn't just a luxury," says author Carl Honoré, a leading advocate of the Slow movement. "It's a mind-set. I hope that [people] will pause and reflect on how they lead their lives and how their lives affect the people and the world around them."

PHOTOGRAPHS
Above: Newcastle, Australia: Justin Aaron
Right: Lisbon, Portugal: Sanda Vuckovic Pagaimo/
Little Upside Down Cake

This year our international hosts, partners and guests have been exploring slow living by cultivating a variety of experiences. In alignment with many of the concepts we explore in *Kinfolk* magazine, our gatherings have included panel discussions, long-table dinners, film screenings, creative collaborations and workspace tours. In Galway, Ireland, guests embraced the concept of slowing down by boating across a lake to where lunch awaited them. Nashville locals got together to hear from Southern makers and creatives whose work embodies the Slow ethos. In Los Angeles, we explored the history and process of coffee through a film screening and partnership with Stumptown Coffee Roasters. In Brussels, we hosted a studio tour and exhibition with a local painter. And in Istanbul, our event hosts arranged a film screening with accompanying scents to take those who attended on a delightful journey of the senses. Regardless of the itinerary, each *Kinfolk* community event treasures the simple but profound act of gathering.

We simply cannot thank our events community around the globe enough for another outstanding series of *Kinfolk* gatherings.

For information on our upcoming events this year and next, please visit us at www.kinfolk.com/events.

ISSUE SEVENTEEN CREDITS

SPECIAL THANKS
Thanks to Katrin Coetzer for the Starters and Family illustrations

ON THE COVER
Photographer Neil Bedford
Styling Aradia Crockett
Hair Amiee Hershan at Stella Creative
Makeup Anne Sophie Costa
Retouching Oliver Carver
Models Earl T. and Emily B. at Nevs
Casting Sarah Bunter
Production We Are Up Production
Special thanks to Thomas Howard

Clothing His T-shirt by COS;
her shirt by Club Monaco

THE FAMILIES WE CHOOSE
Photographer Mikkel Mortensen
Illustrator Christophe Louis

FROM EVERYWHERE AND NOWHERE, TEAM BUILDING, TURNING THE TABLES, OUR GIVEN NAMES & A TREASURE TROVE OF HEIRLOOMS
Illustrator Chidy Wayne

YA'ABURNEE
Special thanks to Sarah Rowland, Adam Baidawi and Karim Mokhtar

THE CREATIVE IMPULSE
Photographer Maia Flore
Special thanks to Baptiste Barbot

A STATE OF SOLITUDE
Photographer Chantal Anderson

MY BEDSIDE TABLE: THE ILLUSTRATOR
Photographer Mikkel Mortensen
Photographer's Assistant Pia Winther
*Special thanks to Illums Bolighus
for the props*

LUNCH AT THE SHOP
Special thanks to Peter Miller

LUNCH BOX RECIPE: WHITE BEAN SOUP WITH GARLIC AND SAUSAGE
Photographer Anders Schønnemann
Food Styling Mikkel Karstad
Prop Styling Sidsel Rudolph
Ceramics Janaki Larsen

THE SOCIAL NETWORK
Prop Styling Rebecca Hernandez
Hair Amiee Hershan at Stella Creative
Makeup Crystabel Riley
Retouching Oliver Carver
Models Raina at Supa and Simian at Elite
Casting Sarah Bunter
Production We Are Up Production
Special thanks to Thomas Howard

Clothing
Page 43: Hat and shirt by COS;
trousers by Folk
Page 44: His sweater by Margaret Howell;
her sweater by Preen
Page 45: T-shirt by Urban Outfitters
Page 46: Shirt by COS; overalls by
Margaret Howell
Page 47: Shirtdress from MHL by
Margaret Howell
Page 48: Shirt by St. James
Page 49: Shirt by Wood Wood
Page 50: Sweater by Joseph
Page 51: Sweater by Margaret Howell

A DAY IN THE LIFE: HUNG-MING CHEN AND CHEN-YEN WEI
Photographer's Assistant Fredrik Bengtsson

MEMORY LANE
Special thanks to Amanda Watters

ARE WE THERE YET?

Grooming Lou Box at S Management
Retouching Oliver Carver
Models George, Harry and Frankie Dawson
at Kids London
Production We Are Up Production
Special thanks to Thomas Howard

Clothing
Page 71: From left: T-shirt and jeans by
American Apparel; boots by Timberland.
T-shirt by Rokit; trousers by Stone Island.
T-shirt by American Apparel; denim shirt,
shorts and sneakers are vintage
Page 74: From left: Sweatshirt by American
Apparel; jeans are vintage. T-shirt by CP
Company; trousers by Stone Island. Sweater
by Wood Wood
Page 76: From left: T-shirt by Rokit.
T-shirt by American Apparel. Trousers are
vintage; boots by Redwing
Page 78: From left: Jeans by American
Apparel. Trousers by Stone Island.
Shorts are vintage
Page 81: From left: T-shirt by American
Apparel. Trousers by Stone Island. T-shirt
by American Apparel; shorts are vintage

LEAN ON ME

Assistant Styling Laurie Lederman
Production Miriam Otterbeck
Models Mario Español and Lj Marles
Movement Director Bret Pfister
Grooming Shukeel Murtaza at
Untitled Artists
*Thanks to Juliet McConnell, FilmFixer
and the residents of the Alexandra and
Ainsworth Estate*

Clothing
Page 97: T-shirt by Jack and Jack; trousers
by COS; shoes by Superga
Sweater by Margaret Howell; trousers
by Jack and Jack; shoes by Superga
Page 98: Top by Joseph; trousers by
Matthew Miller; shoes by Superga
Top by Whistles; jacket, trousers and
belt by J. Lindeberg

Page 99: Sweater by Uniqlo; trousers
by Paul Smith; shoes by Superga
Shirt by Oliver Spencer; trousers by
Tiger of Sweden; shoes by Superga
Page 100–101: Jeans by Lotus;
belt by APC; shoes by Superga
Jeans and belt by J. Lindeberg;
shoes by Superga
Page 102: Jeans by Lotus; belt by APC;
shoes by Superga
Jeans and belt by J. Lindeberg;
shoes by Superga
Page 103: Shirt by COS; trousers
by E. Tautz; shoes by Superga
Shirt by COS; trousers by Sandro;
belt by J. Lindeberg; shoes by Superga
Page 104: Shirt by Sandro; trousers
and belt by J. Lindeberg
Shirt by Filson
Page 105: Shirt by YMC; trousers by
Paul Smith; shoes by Superga
Sweater by Libertine-Libertine; trousers
by Tiger of Sweden; shoes by Superga;
belt by J. Lindeberg

COMMENSALITY

*Special thanks to Ditte Maria Søgaard from
the University of Copenhagen*

MAKING BELIEVE

Photograher's Assistant Wojtek Szauliński
at Szauliński Production
Set Designer Dylan Auman
Hair Miriam Robstad at Bryan
Bantry Agency
Makeup Hanjee at Jet Root
Studio Manager Hazel Kiesewetter at
Candy Studio
Models Helena Greyhorse, Tiffany H.
and Rea at Wilhelmina Models
*Special thanks to Donna Cerutti at
Marek & Associates*

Clothing
Page 111: Shirt by Maryam Nassir Zadeh;
dress by Naadam
Page 113: Shirt is stylist's own; pants by
Phillip Lim; shoes by Maryam Nassir Zadeh
Page 114: Dress by Adam Lippes

Page 115: Shirt is stylist's own; pants by
Maryam Nassir Zadeh
Page 117: Sweater by No. 21
Page 118: Shirt by Maryam Nassir Zadeh;
dress by Naadam
Page 119: Coat by Naadam; tunic by Edun;
skirt by No. 21

THE BLOOD MENU

Food Styling Mikkel Karstad
Prop Styling Sidsel Rudolph
Ceramics Bjarni Sigurdsson

PROFILE SERIES:
THE CREATIVE GENE

*Special thanks to Joanna Bolitho,
Karen Easteal, Gemma Gordon, Vanessa
Haroutunian, Jessica Luo, Sophie Orbaum
and Julia Slack*

NEIGHBORHOOD:
PLAYGROUNDS

Model Michelle Cho

KINFOLK GATHERINGS

*Special thanks to Justin Aaron
and Sanda Vuckovic Pagaimo*